30119 028 786 01 2

CHE
12/10

Managing Separation And Divorce

Diane Roome and Elisabeth Sneade

D1464846

Emerald Guides

Emerald Guides

© Diane Roome and Elisabeth Sneade 2020

Diane Roome and Elisabeth Sneade have asserted the moral right to be identified as the authors of this work.

All rights reserved. No part of this publication may be reproduced in a retrieval system or transmitted by any means, electronic or mechanical, photocopying or otherwise, without the prior permission of the copyright holders.

978-1-913342-77-7

Printed by

4edge www.4edge.co.uk

Whilst every effort has been made to ensure that the information contained within this book is correct at the time of going to press, the author and publisher can take no responsibility for the errors or omissions contained within.

Much has changed in family law from the time we met all those years ago at Staffordshire University as we began our legal studies. What remains true now, as then, is that family law is a 'distress purchase' and rarely do people instruct a family lawyer unless they have a relationship-based query. Our clients tend to be emotional and at the end of a case whilst a 'thank you' would be nice we know that our clients have experienced an emotional journey from the start to end of their case.

We thank Jane McCann for agreeing to write the introduction to this our latest edition of our book. Her knowledge of family law and support for family lawyers and clients in and around Cambridge is much appreciated.

Lastly, we thank our families for their continued support and in particular our little people (Alicia, Isobel and Ruby) for bringing smiles to our faces.

Contents

****

INTRODUCTION

Jane McCann

Counsellor, Mediator, Family Consultant & Divorce Coach

So, you've decided to divorce or separate. Where do you go from here? It's very likely that you will find yourself in a highly emotional state with no idea of where to turn. For most, this is a once in a lifetime experience and certainly not one that is chosen. You might feel utterly overwhelmed about the amount of stuff that needs sorting out. That is to be expected and entirely normal but not easy. How will you tell the children, where will they live? What will you do with the house, how will you fund two separate homes? How will you manage your finances going forwards and how will you get the divorce process started? How will you manage to communicate effectively in order to get the best outcome for the whole family?

Traditionally, separating couples have approached a lawyer in the first instance and this is still a very good option in order to explore the broad picture, to find out what you might be entitled to and how your situation stands in the eyes of the law. However, there are many aspects about divorce and separation that have nothing to do with the law and whilst it is often very helpful to have your own solicitor alongside you, guiding you through the process, there are other professionals who you might find very helpful. Some separating couples do not want to engage a solicitor, either due to cost or to avoid an unnecessary positional approach. Most good family lawyers will do all they can to support you, giving you helpful legal advice along the way as well as introducing you to other professionals as and when appropriate.

It's very important that the right support is sought at the right time. Most separating couples benefit from accessing a mix of legal, financial and emotional support. This differs from case to case, it's about what you as individuals or a family need or choose.

Financial advisers are the best placed people to help you navigate your way through anything to do with property and finance - this might include helping you work out your expenditure, giving advice about mortgage providers, exploring options for what you might do with your pensions as well as giving you invaluable advice regarding businesses, tax and more besides. They are also very helpful in helping you implement the outcomes of any financial settlement such as pension orders. It's very important that you seek the support of an independent financial adviser who can provide neutral input either for you as an individual or as a couple.

You may well be struggling with managing your emotions at this difficult time and it can be very helpful to seek support from a counsellor who can help prepare you to be emotionally ready for what's to come. Many couples separate due to a breakdown of communication and yet, when children are involved, this is the very time when communication is of paramount importance. Family Consultants or Divorce Coaches (generally from a therapeutic background), can guide you through the process as well as giving you invaluable guidance about issues associated with children and communication, helping you transition from partners to co-operative co-parents. They can also help you process difficult, often embittered feelings you may have and enhance your skills to deal with the practicalities.

The most important thing to remember is that this is your process, that you are in the driving seat and that it's your choice to decide who to access to provide the most helpful, cost-effective support to get through this. Members of Resolution, be they lawyers, financial advisers, mediators or family consultants, should all be able to lay out your options and introduce you to a team of professionals that will work together to help you achieve the very best outcome.

Jane McCann
Mediator, Family Consultant & Counsellor
www.janemccann.co.uk

Chapter 1

Sorting Out the Emotional Stuff

It hurts where you are right now

When you separate from a partner, managing the emotional impact on you is a priority. Failure to address it can prove to be extremely costly in both financial and personal terms. However your separation came about, make no mistake; you will experience an emotional response. Don't be surprised as even if you separate on good terms you will still feel the effects of splitting from your partner.

We are not psychologists. The purpose of this chapter is to help you identify what is happening to you and to give consideration to seeking professional guidance to help you manage yourself, your feelings and the situation you find yourself in. We cannot change what has happened between you and your ex, but you can move forwards. It will take time and effort but you can do it!

You have a responsibility to yourself and your family, especially your children, to address your feelings about the split. It is perfectly normal to experience a whole range of emotional responses when the decision to separate from a partner is made. The trick is to acknowledge that your feelings are a natural human response to the situation you are in, and then to deal with them, with or without professional help – that bit is up to you.

The potential costs if you don't

If you want to spend an hour in tears on the phone to your lawyer they will no doubt be extremely sympathetic BUT THEY WILL CHARGE YOU for that time! As this is likely to be a minimum of £250 per hour so that is an extremely expensive phone call. You can do the maths – it won't take long to have a £1,500 plus bill if you spend time offloading your upset to your lawyer who will not be a therapist and therefore not able to help you with your feelings.

Then consider your friends and family. They will be kind, supportive and prepared to listen. But they can only do so much. Do not risk alienating them by passing on your distress to them. Even if you have a friend or relative with a professional qualification (e.g. psychologist, counsellor) we would suggest you consider seeing someone you don't know and is one step removed as the therapeutic relationship can then remain purely professional.

Separation affects more than 2 people

Think about your family and the people the split will affect. If we take a couple with 2 children and grandparents, then 8 people will be involved.

Children

Mum and Dad

Grandparents

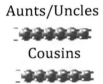

Then there will be aunts, uncles and cousins. By this stage 20 people are in the affected group.

Aunts/Uncles

Cousins

Consider additional friends; say 3 couples, all of whom have 2 children. Then 12 more people are added to the group which by now totals 32 people.

Mum and Dad's friends

Mum and Dad's friend's children

We haven't even started to look at work colleagues, school friends and their parents. Some will be close to you and your ex, and they may be uncomfortable and worried about appearing to be disloyal to you or your ex. They will not want to 'take sides'. If you have supportive and caring friends and family do you want to risk losing those relationships by forcing them to choose between you?

Can I do this on my own?

There are no right or wrong answers here. Be honest with yourself about how you feel and whether you are strong enough to deal with these feelings. There is absolutely no shame at all in admitting that you are struggling. It is alright to not be ok.

Try considering the questions in the short questionnaire we have put together and then look at these answers to consider whether you want to seek additional help and support.

Questionnaire

This questionnaire is designed to help yourself identify whether you can effectively manage your emotions following your separation. If not, then could you benefit from some professional help?

1. How do I feel about myself?

    a) Am I distressed?

    b) Am I angry?

    c) Do I feel abandoned or rejected?

    d) Do I feel guilty?

e) Do I blame them for the split?

f) Do I blame myself for the split?

g) Who do I feel is responsible for the separation?

2. How do I behave when I see and speak to my ex?

   a) Politely, with respect and objectively?

   b) Am I accusatory, angry and blaming them for what has happened?

   c) Can I speak to them clearly and convey my point with clarity?

   d) Am I very emotional and tearful?

3. Do I trust my ex

   a) With money?

   b) With the children's care and well-being?

   c) To be straightforward and honest with me

If you have answered 'yes' to any of the above questions we suggest that you seek additional help and support.

Managing Anger- Yours or your Ex's

Here are some tips for managing anger whether it's yours or your ex's.

- Get professional help if you need to
- Take responsibility for your part in the break-up
- Learn what pushes buttons – try to identify and understand what makes you angry
- Learn what pushes your ex's buttons – do you need to modify your own behaviour towards them?
- Be compassionate to both of you. You cannot change what has happened. Don't beat up yourself or your ex because of what has taken place.
- Be honest with yourself. If someone is angry with you, ask yourself why. Is there something in it?
- Be brave and take a break then return to the discussion when things have calmed down.
- Try not to take it personally - anger is a projection of one's feelings. It is their own turmoil which often leads to a person being angry.
- Forgive, let it go and move on. Do you want a future that is happy and fulfilled? Then let it go. Remember Catullus who wrote "I love and I hate. How can I do this you may ask? I don't, but it is excruciating and I am in hell"

Don't spend your life living negatively. If the covid pandemic has shown us anything it is that life is short and unpredictable!.

Where to look for help

Try your GP. They can signpost you or refer you to relevant services in your area. Some GP's are able to offer initial counselling sessions at a relatively low cost and sometimes it is free to begin with.

British Association for Counselling & Psychotherapy 01455 883300 bacp@bacp.co.uk

Twitter: @BACP

Gingerbread 0207 428 5400 http://www.gingerbread.org.uk/

Relate 0300 100 1234 http://www.relate.org.uk/

Communication

Poor communication is often at the root of problems between separated couples.

We cannot emphasise enough how important it is that you communicate effectively-particularly where arrangements for children are concerned.

Modern life is busy, often frenetic, and we live in an age where technology rules our means of communicating with each other. When we first wrote this book a handful of people had smart phones but now most people (and even children) have iPhone, chrome books or iPads. The speed with which we communicate can be both a blessing and a curse. The sheer immediacy of these methods of communication can mean that we don't think through what we are saying, and how we express it. This can sometimes cause difficulties.

Three key features to improve your communication:-

A) Speak or write plainly (but not rudely!). Remember that the recipient might try to read between the lines so make sure what you are trying to say is clear.

B) Don't bury your point in other stuff, particularly old arguments or upsets. Think bullet points and not and essay that you're trying to write!

C) Listen to each other. Careful listening is a key skill. Take note of the language the other person is using. Try not to look for a hidden agenda – not only will you miss the point, but you will also cause yourself unnecessary anguish.

D) "Engage brain" first! Think through what you want to say or read through a message a couple of times before responding. If it is a tricky topic draft the message and leave it for an hour then go back and review what you have written.

10 Tips for effective communication with your ex

1. Always be respectful. You loved each other once. If you have children they will always be part of your life. This is a situation you cannot change.

2. Keep your discussions factual. Use clear language without ambiguity. Ask direct questions e.g. "will you take the children to their swimming lesson on Saturday please?"

3. Do not start to apportion blame or look for answers you are unlikely to receive. For example, "why won't you ever take the children swimming?" or "you prefer to go to the match rather than take the children swimming," are

unlikely to produce a positive response and are much more likely to trigger an argument.

4. Do not have a detailed conversation when handing children over after a visit. Keep your conversation friendly and positive for the children's benefit.

5. When you need to have that detailed discussion make arrangements for:-

- A mutually convenient time;

- Set aside a neutral venue away from the family home if possible;

- Set an agenda and remember you both have valid points to discuss;

- Keep a note of any points agreed to avoid misunderstandings later;

- If this sounds like you are planning for a business meeting then it might help to think of it this way.

6. Do not worry if you disagree. That's life! If you were still together as a couple you would not agree on everything. It's ok to disagree but the trick is to manage disagreements and find a compromise or to agree to disagree.

7. Allow each other the opportunity to air your views. Don't shout each other down, and DO NOT swear or speak abusively to each other.

8. If you use email or text try not to be too curt as these methods of communication can be misunderstood as for example, a request can be interpreted as a demand!

9. Don't forget your ex may not respond to your text or email immediately, be patient.

10. Avoid discussing your ex on social networking sites. In our experience these discussions frequently find their way back to the subject of the 'chat'.

Not only does this lead to problems between adults but can impact negatively on children as their friends or their friends' parents may have seen and passed on the details.

Be prepared

There are various points during the separation process when you should be prepared to feel upset. The list below is by no means prescriptive, and we cannot guarantee there will not be other times when you will feel particularly emotional, but they do seem to be trigger factors common to many people.

1. When we receive any court papers, let's face it, to have something such as your personal relationship details set out formally on court documents can be pretty chilling. The details may not look very pretty set down in black

and white. Remember these documents are part of the process.

2. When looking at your financial position this may be uncomfortable. You are splitting one pot of money between you so measures such as downsizing your home or cutting back on regular expenditure may be necessary. Remember we can live without satellite TV or gym membership at least for a while. Prioritise the essential spending and be prepared to consider cheaper alternatives to everything.

3. Telling the children, family and friends can be hard. If you can tell the child together with the other parent then not only does this mean you are supporting each other, but you are also sharing the responsibility. (There is more about how to tell the children in the chapter on children).

4. When you attend the formal meetings whether with your lawyer or mediator it is useful to take information with you in writing. (See the chapter on finances for a list of the information the lawyers will need).

****

Main Points from Chapter One

Sorting Out the Emotional Stuff

➤ When you separate from a partner, managing the emotional impact on you, and others, is a priority. Failure to address it can prove extremely costly in both personal and financial terms.

➤ Separation affects more than 2 people-think about your family and the people the split will affect.

➤ There are a number of places where you can look for help-your GP, Counsellors, Relate and others.

➤ Be prepared-there are various points along the separation process where you should be prepared to feel upset.

➤ Effective communication is key to managing matters, particularly arrangements for children.

****

Chapter 2

Assessing What You Want to Achieve

Once you are sure your relationship is over it is well worthwhile taking stock of what you want to achieve.

The key question to ask yourself at the outset is "what would I do if I was in my ex's shoes?" The earlier you can do this, the sooner you will be able to enter into negotiations positively and arrive at a mutually acceptable solution. Remember though that until you are emotionally ready to move forward trying to resolve the financial arrangements or agree how often the children will see each parent will be difficult.

There are a number of 'deadly' obstacles to negotiation which are not too far removed from the deadly sins! Don't let any of these apply to you as they are likely to incur significant emotional and financial costs!

- Anger will simply waste time and energy.
- Jealousy will be counterproductive. It gets you nowhere and remember you are no longer in a relationship with the other person.

- Greed makes any form of reasonable negotiation impossible.
- Pride results in statements. Let go of your principles and be practical.
- Lust will just get in the way- if it is well and truly over stay focused on sorting out solutions.
- Fear can be the worst enemy of productive negotiations.
- Separation and divorce is a very difficult time and fear of the unknown can be a very effective blocker to moving on.

Remember there are options for both of you. Focus on the problem, not the person. Be practical and realistic- you may have loved the family home but if you can't afford it on your own is it realistic to stay there? It is the people who make a home – if you've built one you can build another. Be flexible where possible. We have seen many people disappointed and upset if they set their heart on another property before the family home has been sold. Vendors will sell properties to those who are in a position to pay them. So whilst it is useful to acquire knowledge of the housing market and the costs of renting or buying, try not to be seduced by a particular house as you may be disappointed.

Think about taking some legal advice at this stage. It is important that you know what can be achieved legally. In England and Wales some major legal changes are due to come into force. The Divorce, Dissolution and Separation Bill will be enacted in the autumn of 2021, and couples will be able to make a "no fault" application to divorce. Joint applications will be allowed, and the ability to contest an application for divorce will be removed.

The intention behind these long awaited changes is to encourage those who have decided their relationship is at an end to sever the legal tie between them without acrimony or unnecessary expense. The entire process can now be completed online, without the need to attend court, provided financial arrangements are settled.

Questions before negotiation:

Ask yourself the following questions prior to any negotiation:

1) List the top 5 things you want to achieve from your separation and why you have listed them
2) List 5 things you think the other person wants to get out of the process and why
3) What are your 5 greatest worries and why are they of concern
4) What do you think the other persons 5 greatest worries are and why?
5) What are your goals for yourself and your children at the conclusion of the process?
6) Work out for yourself, with your answers to the previous questions in mind, the following:

   o The most you would be willing to give or give up
   o The least you would be willing to give or give up

7) The bottom line you would be willing to agree upon. Do some homework. Look at the alternative costs of housing – e.g. mortgage costs or monthly rental costs and have a look at some other properties. It can be a useful exercise if only to rule out some options as unaffordable. Work out what you spend each month at the moment and where it would be possible to make savings. Drawing up a monthly budget is an especially helpful exercise. Your proposals need to be both realistic and achievable, and a budget is a key piece of information which will help you with this.

8) Avoid treating everything as of equal importance. Don't get hung up over the last 5 glasses in the cupboard.

9) Is there a solution you can live with?

>THINK   'acceptable' not 'fair'
>
>   'how' not 'why'
>
>   'problem' not 'person'
>
>   'achievable' not 'principle'

10) Consider taking legal advice at this stage. It is important that you are fully aware of the legal framework for your decisions.

Now read the main points from Chapter 2 overleaf.

****

Main points from Chapter 2

Assessing What You Want to Achieve

➤ Once you are sure your relationship is over, it is well worthwhile taking stock of what you want to achieve.

➤ There are a number of "deadly obstacles" to negotiation- but don't let them apply to you, as they are likely to incur significant emotional and financial costs

➤ Consider taking legal advice at this stage. You need to know the legal implications of your decisions. Up to date knowledge and advice is important.

****

Chapter 3

Finances

Immediate needs, paying the bills, assessing priority payments

One of the first issues to think about when separating is who is going to pay the bills and rent or mortgage and what must be paid immediately to avoid further problems developing at a later date. If you can agree quickly who will pay the bills it will then give you both time to breath and then identify what you would like to achieve long term.

It's not uncommon for people to have very little day-to-day knowledge of their own finances. Quite often family life inevitably means one person takes the lead on different things, whether they be finances, practical day-to-day arrangements for the children or even who puts the bins out! So, when separating make sure you familiarise yourself with the key financial elements of your own life. Think about the following:

i) do you know where the bank accounts are and know the current balances?
ii) do you know who your mortgage is with and how much you owe?

iii) who has credit cards or other debts?

iv) do you know what you both earn?

If you cannot agree who is going to pay the mortgage then you will very quickly find yourself dealing with red letters arriving in the post and that only adds to what is already a stressful situation. The more non-payment of bills takes place the fewer options you will find available to you in terms of credit being offered which could then take away your preferred financial settlement.

If you are thinking in terms of you or your spouse taking on the current mortgage rather than selling the house for goodness sake prioritise payment of the mortgage otherwise you may find that you are considered a 'bad risk'. What are the important bills to be paid? Each case will vary but listed below are the top priorities in most cases.

Housing – who is going to pay the mortgage or rent?

Will you pay half each or will one of you pay this and the other pay for something else? Much will depend on whether you are both going to stay living in the house until you have reached an agreement about finances. If one of you is moving out it will probably be the case that the person staying at the house will pay the mortgage or rent.

There may be help available to you in the short term. Think about talking to your lender about arranging to pay less in the short term to give yourself some breathing space, but remember this could affect your credit rating. Perhaps your lender will agree to you switching to an interest only mortgage for a short time?

The key thing is to talk to your lender as soon as you can to find out your options and then you can make some decisions.

Wherever you live, and it sounds obvious, make sure that you prioritise paying for your home! If you are in rented accommodation you may qualify for state benefits to help you meet the cost of your rent. Talk to your rental agency if you think payments could be erratic in the short-term.

<u>Childcare</u> – if you both work and are going to keep working how will you pay for childcare? If you are separated from your spouse or partner you may now qualify for state benefits (tax credits) to help reduce the cost of childcare. Many parents find that the cost of childcare is a large percentage of one parent's income. When you separate, the parent with whom the children lives may find that once they have paid for childcare there is nothing left to pay for the mortgage or rent, let alone buy food and pay all of the other day-to-day bills.

Try to agree early on how this cost will be met, particularly if both of you are going to continue working. Also give consideration to how childcare costs during the school holidays will be paid. When one parent works school hours the need for childcare is often largely out of sight as it tends to be only at

31

Easter, Christmas and the summer holidays that this cost becomes a problem. Can family members or friends help out, or do you have enough holidays between the two of you to cover this time with the children? Perhaps there is a holiday club that could provide the childcare that you need? If so, how will the holiday club be paid for?

Other debts such as credit cards, car finances, unsecured loans

Most of us will owe money, other than for our mortgage, in a variety of forms whether that be a car loan, a home improvement loan to do up the kitchen or some other house-based project, or money spent on our credit cards for those items we wanted but didn't have the cash at the time to afford. It is not unusual for clients to meet with their lawyers and have in excess of £10k owing on credit cards plus other loans too. Very often if you are meeting the loan repayments comfortably out of your joint income it is easy to forget what a drain on individual finances these payments can be when/if you have to pay it out of one income.

It is often not until couples separate that the repayments become an issue. If you find that making the monthly payments is going to be tricky when you separate, be upfront with your creditors. They would much prefer to receive the money you owe over more months, than you default. Keep your creditors in the loop and make minimum payments if necessary. If you miss payments it will affect your credit rating and may make it more difficult to secure other financing later on.

Household bills

It is easy to miss the different expenses involved in running a home. It is often not until you have to face meeting those costs out of a sole income having paid for them jointly that you realise how many different bills there are to pay. Write a list and decide which of your current expenses you need to continue to have. Is it vital, for example, that you have the all-singing-all-dancing Sky package? Could you have Freeview instead? Can you reduce your food bill or switch your utility bills to a different supplier to save costs? Think of the costs involved and whether you can continue your current lifestyle. Two incomes to run one household is very a different proposition!

Checklist for drawing up monthly budget

Where do you start? Prepare a monthly budget to see what your costs are. Look at the Summary of Expenditure in the Appendix for an example. Separate your costs out into:-

- Housing
- Car running costs
- Domestic expenses
- Personal expenses
- Replacement items
- Costs associated with your children

Next, be honest with yourself. If you are spending beyond your means take decisive action to cut your costs. Change your shopping habits, use online resources to get better deals from your utility providers and cut down on the frivolous spending. Do you really need a coffee each lunch time? Could you use that £10 in a more constructive way? Make the most of the online voucher schemes and comparison websites. Martin Lewis has a website, moneysavingexpert.com that is a great place to start your research.

Although it is time-consuming and rather dull to sit and work out your budget shortly after your separation if you prioritise this you will save time and money in the long run. One of the first things your lawyer is going to need to know from you is what are the priority bills that need to be paid and who is going to pay them? In addition, the information contained in the mass of paperwork you will sift through when putting together your budget is not lost time. The information will be needed by the other professionals, such as financial advisors, throughout your case.

Remember that the best way to reduce your legal and other costs is to be organised and provide the information asked for by your representatives swiftly. If you have already agreed your budget and worked out how your monthly expenses are going to be met when you separate into two households you will have saved a great deal of time and therefore money.

Where to go for help with debt

There are many organisation that offer help to those who are struggling to pay their debts. Being upfront with those that you owe money to is the priority.

The CAB offer debt advice www.citizensadvice.org/int/debt-and-money as do many charities such as Step Change http://www.stepchange.org

Try to avoid, if you can, debt management companies who charge an administration fee for dealing with your debts as that may well add to your money worries rather than help.

The Money Advice Service www.moneyadviceservice.org.uk is government based but established in conjunction with a family lawyer and is another useful resource.

Some mortgage companies may be willing to consider a 'mortgage holiday' period which means you pay a nothing or a reduced rate for a short period. This may give you time to agree what is going to happen longer term to the family home and reach a long-term settlement.

If you try to reach a quick agreement because both of you are very aware that you only have enough money to pay the next 2 months' mortgage you will often feel resentful later on that you rushed into those decisions. Can you 'restructure' your debt in the short term? For example, could you consolidate several outstanding credit card debts into one loan that is easier to manage? Make sure that you are always paying off the debt with the highest rate of interest first as your priority (in addition to paying your housing costs) and then work your way down your list to the next highest interest paying debt and so on.

Information the professionals will need – using a checklist based on what the court may need if you litigate will save time later on

In addition to a completed summary of expenditure the professionals involved in your case whether they be lawyers, financial advisors or someone else are all going to want to see similar documentation. If you gather everything together at the outset you will help yourself get the advice you need as soon as possible. You will also save time as the professionals will not have to wait to advise you about a particular issue until they have all of your information to hand. So, what will they need?

1. A valuation of the family home or confirmation of your current tenancy agreement;
2. Your most recent mortgage statement;
3. Your last 6 months wage slips together with your P60 and P11D, (if you have one);
4. Copies of bank statements for the last 12 months for each bank account;
5. If you run your own business copies of your most recent profit and loss accounts (if possible covering the past 2 years) and if your business accountant is able to give you an idea about what your business is worth and whether

you could borrow any money secured against your business that might be helpful too;

6. Details of any state benefits you receive;

7. A list of the other assets you have such as endowment policies, savings, shares;

8. A list of the other liabilities you have such as unsecured loans and credit cards;

9. Your most recent pension statement and confirmation of how much state pension you are scheduled to receive;

10. Confirmation of your mortgage capacity;

11. Details of alternative housing options on a purchase and rental basis together with any special requirements such as a map showing school catchment areas.

Now read the main points from Chapter 3 overleaf.

****

Main Points from Chapter 3

Finances

➤ One of the first issues to think about when separating is to agree who is going to pay the bills and which ones must be paid immediately.

➤ If you can agree at the outset who is going to pay the bills, it will give you both time to breathe and plan for the longer term.

➤ It is very important to prioritise the bills-for example housing and childcare payments.

➤ Prepare a monthly budget so you can see clearly what your costs are.

➤ If you are struggling to pay debts, there are many organisations in existence that offer help and advice.

****

Chapter 4

In Business Together?

What to do if you run a business together when you separate?

Many couples find themselves wanting to separate but feeling as though they cannot do so. Maybe you run a building business together (generally he will be doing the building and she will be sorting out the 'book's and most of the admin) or maybe it is a shop based or office based business and one person is the front of house and the other one does the back-office tasks. The fear when one person decides that the relationship is at an end is if they were to leave how could they do so and not destroy the business that has provided the family overall with income.

A former client, who asked to remain nameless, has managed to achieve what we can only refer to as a 'good separation'. That is not to say they managed to separate without feeling sad, angry or making mis-steps along the way. (Him telling the children they were separating because of 'her' behaviour' was a low point). However, several months after the Decree Absolute was granted and the financial order approved they are able to continue to run the business together that they have built up over the last 20 years. Fast forward several years and they continue to co-parent their now adult children as well as they can but crucially she recognises that this was only possible with 3 things all coming into line:-

1. Her determination not to walk away from the business as it has provided them both with a good income and will continue to do so;
2. The constant help and support of an honest family consultant (See Jane's introduction as to why she and anyone else like her can add to a tricky emotional time); and
3. Recognition by her (less so by him who is less emotionally aware) that there will continue to be bumps along the way but looking at the big picture is vital. This continues to be accurate several years after their separation.

So what are the common issues that couples who work together will face?

You will may have staff members that work alongside you and your partner. Being honest with those who work alongside you about your separation is vital. They won't want to get caught up in your personal struggles. Staff members want assurance that they will have a job in the short and medium term.

If you separate part-way through an accounting period think about the practical impact that there would be if you were to close your partnership/business. Meet with your accountant sooner rather than later to get their input about your options. If you really cannot continue to work together what is the most painless way to close things down? Advice from your business accountant is going to be vital. It could be that the business is a partnership and there are more partners than you can manage. A limited company has even more issues to be aware of. If there are shareholders and directors that's an added complication too. Planning ahead is really important and your company accountant is best placed to help you. Don't make life difficult for the person who decides they wish to walk away from the business. Make sure that everyone is able to file their tax returns and don't withhold paperwork that they might need to exit the business smoothly. Shouting might make you feel good in the short-term but longer term it has a tendency to backfire.

There are so many issues that arise as a result of a decision to separate and negotiating your way through the divorce process and dealing with your children and the emotional fall-out is hard enough. However, when you have the added stress of knowing that your relationship ending is impacting those you work with too that adds a feeling of responsibility like no other.

Once no longer married, if you decide to work together beyond divorce will you have a shareholders agreement? Will you change the business banking arrangements? Will the way that salaries get paid need to change? Sometimes in person might not receive a salary as is it has been paid into the 'family pot' so that will need to change. The list goes on and each business is bespoke and has a different set of challenges. However, you know your own business best so trust in your ability to make the decision that are right for your business and also your family too.

If you decide to run the business until the end of your next tax-year or beyond your separation you really need your accountant to ensure that tax returns get filed properly and you are both putting away money that previously might have been managed by one of you to pay both tax bills. Those things might now be more of an individual responsibility post-separation.

Most importantly 'put a business head on' when making decisions. That isn't always easy. You might be on a site visit with your soon to be divorced other half and one of you receives a call from school to say that your little person has hurt themselves or feels poorly and needs to be collected. Pre-separation that would been dealt with and there would be no politics. Now, post-separation there will invariably be trickiness when home and work collide. If you have teenagers rather than little people then you may also have their emotional outbursts to deal with too so try your best to keep a level head.

If you run a small business you may find yourself suddenly without any support at home as you have separated from your partner, but equally you have no support at work either as your co-business owner is your soon to be ex-partner. Use your network of friends and family to ensure you have as much support as you can find.

If you have run a business together for a long time there might be company cars that you own. If you have always been the admin one and the person that sorted out car insurance, tax etc. then you'll be ok. Remember the other person might have no idea what needs to be sorted and if you are separating they will need support to ensure that the car they continue to drive around in is taxed, insured etc.

Aside from our example lady, who has continued to run a business post-divorce with her former husband, there are many examples of others that have done the same. Running a family business is incredibly common. Having respect for the value that your former partner adds to the business is important.

The anger will initially be the driving emotion but with continued support from a family counselor during the initial period of separation, and afterwards, when perhaps the role of the family counselor changes to being more of a business coach, those conversations continue to be important.

Clear communication enables better productivity for the couple that were once living together but also for the team members too. Remember- as we talk about earlier on in this book- the impact of your separation is wide-spread. If you run a business together the fall-out is felt far wider than your initial family. The potential instability that you create, not just for your own family, but all of those other families where one person works in your business is widespread.

With time, the anger hopefully turns to acceptance and with the help of a specialist counselor that enables you both to communicate in a more positive way. It is vital to stop the behaviour of employees 'picking sides'. That can create chaos and isn't a helpful atmosphere for the business. Depending on the size and nature of your business you may need to bring in external help from a counselor to enable your employees to be clear about the future direction of your business and how the changes you are putting in place in your personal relationship are going to impact the business in the short, medium and longer term.

In the end, the decision is one for you both to make. You decided to run a business together for good reasons. Maybe the question to ask is whether those initial decisions still remain - irrespective of the fact that you will no longer be living together? With good communication co-running a business is possible. The question of whether they will do so remains. Our example lady has said that she intends to use her specialist counselor in the longer term to enable her working and business life changes to co-exist. To quote her directly 'we all need a healthy working life as well'. If we could only tell you what our example lady and her now ex-husband have achieved post separation with her business you would be amazed.

Now read the main points from Chapter 4 overleaf.

****

Main Points from Chapter Four

In Business Together?

➢ Many couples find themselves wanting to separate but feeling as though they cannot do so because of a joint business venture.

➢ The fear when one person decides that the relationship is at an end is if they were to leave how could they do so and not destroy the business that has provided the family overall with income.

➢ You will probably have staff members that work alongside you and your partner. Being honest with those who work alongside you about your separation is vital. They won't want to get caught up in your personal struggles. Staff members want assurance that they will have a job in the short and medium term.

➢ Advice from your business accountant is going to be vital. It could be that the business is a partnership and there are more partners than you can manage. A limited company has even more issues to be aware of. If there are shareholders and directors that's an added complication too. Planning ahead is really important and your company accountant is best placed to help you.

****

Chapter 5

Who the Professionals Are and What They Do

When you instruct a lawyer very often you think that you will be the only one to deal with them. Whilst many years ago that was certainly the case nowadays lawyers work closely with a range of other professionals to offer their clients the best service to meet their individual needs. The professionals most commonly used are:-

1. The lawyers
2. Financial advisors
3. Actuaries
4. Mediators
5. Family counsellors/Family Consultants
6. Estate agents
7. GPs
8. Accountants/Tax specialists/Arbitrators

The lawyers

Your lawyer will always be your first point of call. It is the lawyer who is instructed by you to resolve your divorce and/or financial issues following your separation. A good lawyer will identify early on where other professionals will be needed and delegate specific tasks within your case to them at relevant points. Your lawyer can provide you with all of the legal advice but they cannot and must not advise you about other issues outside the area of their expertise. For example, your lawyer cannot tell you what your mortgage capacity is going to be or calculate how much of your pension you should transfer to your husband or wife. These tasks must be delegated to the specialists as both of these have huge financial implications if calculated incorrectly.

Your lawyer may work on a fixed-fee or per-hour basis. Be clear at the outset what is and is not covered in their costs. Will you have to pay to speak to their secretary or not? How much money do they want from you 'up front'? Can you pay monthly or set up a standing order? Will you be charged for photocopying? Are you able to obtain a litigation loan? Most financial statements are 100+ pages long. So, will the lawyer that you meet be doing all of the work or will they pass the more straightforward tasks to junior members of their team? What is the hourly rate you will be charged? Remember, lawyers tend to calculate their charges in 6 minute units so each email you send them will be 1 unit, each response another 6 minutes. Very quickly that time adds up and we tend to say to our clients that picking up the telephone is nearly always more cost effective. Emails are a great way to set out a list of things that you want to discuss but if you have questions and you think there will be some back and forth pick up the phone otherwise your costs could be far higher than you originally budgeted. In the past, firms might agree that a client could pay their legal costs when the family home sold meaning your lawyers waited to be paid until the end of your case. Nowadays it is rare for law firms to do this. 'Cash is King' in the legal business, meaning that many firms will bill you monthly and say that if invoices are unpaid for more than a month no further work will be done on your case. In our case we tend to say to clients that with two invoices outstanding we 'put our pens down' and if explained at the outset everyone is clear on the basis that you are operating. Realistically you wouldn't expect a tradesman to work without interim bills being paid and buying legal advice is no different. You may also be charged interest on any outstanding balance. More firms now offer fixed fees which means that you as the client has certainty and can plan how you are going to pay your legal bills. A fixed fee option might not be advertised but ask.

Where do you find your lawyer? Personal recommendation is always best. If someone has acted for a friend or family member and they did a good job you will be more inclined to use them than an unknown person. Many family lawyers are members of Resolution and you can search their website for lawyers in your local area: www.resolution.org.uk).

If a lawyer is a member of Resolution it means that they will abide by the Resolution Code of Conduct so that negotiations are carried out in as non-confrontational a way possible. Your needs as the client are prioritised over sending vitriolic letters. More importantly, it is recognised that where there are children involved, their needs will be at the centre of all discussions.

You can also use the 'find a solicitor' search function on the Law Society website www.lawsociety.org.uk and our top tip is that if you telephone a lawyer and they won't talk to you for 5 minutes or so about how they work then you're probably going to find it difficult to get through to them if they were your lawyer and you needed a question answering. Choose someone that you find is approachable and with whom you feel comfortable

The Financial Advisors (IFA's)

Most people will know of a financial advisor who has helped a friend or family member but many people do not have a designated IFA. Lawyers will have good links with the local financial advisors and should be able to recommend several in your area who can help.

Why do you need a financial advisor? Not all clients do. Most people come into contact with IFAs when setting up a pension, sorting out life insurance or managing your investments. Some IFA's are now specially trained in family law to enable them to better work alongside family lawyers. Some also have recognition as being a PODE (Pension on Divorce Expert) as pensions are a tricky area when couples separate. This means that they have an understanding of how the law works and a view of how the Court would treat your case if it went to a contested hearing. Resolution has a detailed exam and those IFAs who want to be seen as a 'divorce specialist' are able to take this. Details of IFA's who have the experience to give advice on family cases can be found on the Resolution website under the 'find a member' section.

Your lawyer will probably ask you to meet with an IFA if you are thinking about having your former partner's pension transferred in part to you or vice versa. The IFA will be able to explain how much money you are likely to receive after a transfer takes place. The general rule is that where there is a pension asset worth more than £100,000 you certainly ought to meet with an IFA as the decisions you make when you divorce can impact your retirement plans.

Another less well-known function that a financial advisor can perform is helping to bring people quickly up to speed with their financial admin. Very often one half of the couple has been charged with 'dealing with the money'. This tends to mean the other person has little or no clue about what money is where, or even who their mortgage company is. An IFA will quickly be able to help that person gather the knowledge and answer any questions they have so that they are then confident to firstly, tell their lawyer what they want to achieve, and secondly, do not feel like they are unclear when discussing financial issues with their former partner. Knowledge is power as they say!

Lastly, IFA's are great at cash flow modelling which means that they are able to look at what your monthly outgoings are and then run the numbers to estimate what you will need either in terms of a lump sum settlement or perhaps as maintenance from your former partner. This information can be really helpful to either 'sense-check' and offer you have received from your former partner or to enable you to put forward an offer that really meets your needs and is fair.

Actuaries (aka the number geeks)

Most people have pensions and, when they separate, those pensions remain a matrimonial asset that is divided just as the equity in a house or money in a bank account. The difference is that a pension is invested for many years and is often linked to the stock market making it very difficult to predict how much it is worth now and in several years ahead.

Given that many people move jobs frequently compared to previous generations it is also quite common for people to have more than one pension. The value of a pension can be at times far greater than the house equity, especially if a pension has been running for 10-15 years! Make sure that all of the pension pots are disclosed. If there are final salary pensions involved or perhaps one of you has a Teacher's pension or NHS fund they can be really tricky so make sure you get the right advice before making any decisions. When dealing with pensions broadly there are three approaches.

1. You can decide that you both keep your own pensions and other assets may be offset to deal with any imbalance in your pension provision.
2. Alternatively, you can equalise pension investments meaning that you both have the same amount invested in your pensions following your divorce. (This approach tends to be less used nowadays)
3. Lastly, you can share your pensions so that you equalise the pension income you will both receive on retirement age.

A lawyer cannot do the complicated calculation to work out how much of one pension should be transferred to another person in order to equalise pensions. That is the role of an actuary.

Complicating factors such as your respective ages, health factors and the specific pension investments that you each have are relevant factors. Actuaries tend to be instructed jointly so that you both share in the cost of paying for their advice. It may feel like you are paying a lot of money for a calculation to be carried out and to some extent this is true. However, over a number or years the difference between 1% and 2% of pension can make a real difference when planning for your retirement. So, paying for this expert opinion if your lawyer suggests it as a sensible step forwards is nearly always a wise thing to do. Remember if you are involved in court proceedings the judge might want an expert report to be able to make a decision in your case if you have not been able to reach agreement.

There are many actuaries who specialise in carrying out the specialist calculations with pensions in divorce cases. Your lawyer should be able to tell you who to instruct and give you an idea of likely cost. Remember that the costs of the Actuary report is usually shared between you.

Mediators

Mediators act as an impartial third party between you and your ex to facilitate your discussions in trying to reach consensus between you. Mediation is voluntary, although is a requirement that before anyone makes an application to Court that a referral to mediation is made. It may be that you have dealings with a Mediator on an assessment basis who then decides that you and your former partner do need the Court to help you resolve your disputes. Other couples though find Mediation a useful venue to resolve their disputes.

The idea of Mediation is that you and your former partner use the process to negotiate towards a final agreement (whether that be in terms of your financial issues or children's arrangements) with the mediator being the neutral third party keeping things as calm as possible and on-track towards a negotiated settlement. Mediation is a means of problem- solving

A mediator works alongside your lawyer as although they may be a lawyer, not all mediators are. Mediators are able to tell you the sort of settlements that a Court would accept but they cannot go into detail about whether a particular proposal is the right one for you to accept. That remains the role of your lawyer. A Mediator should flag up for you key points when it would be useful to seek legal advice.

As a way of resolving your disputes mediation is competitive in terms of cost and time as not only do mediators tend to charge less per hour than your respective lawyers, they are able to have meetings as and when it suits you and your former partner. For example, if you both agree you want to meet every week until you have an agreement there is nothing to stop you doing so.

Mediators come from a wide variety of backgrounds and, like lawyers, will work closely alongside IFA's and other specialists. We would recommend you choose a mediator who is registered with the Family Mediation Council (if using a mediator in England and Wales). These mediators follow a code of practice established by the FMC and have received a high standard of training and assessment. For more information go to the Family Mediation Website familymediationcouncil.org.uk. For a limited number of cases there is still public funding (legal aid) available to cover the cost of mediation. Some organisations offer a sliding scale of charges depending upon your income so look at what is on offer in your local area and compare how the mediators near to you charge for their time.

Family Counsellors/Consultants/Therapists

Frequently, as lawyers, our clients will talk to us about issues that are not strictly part of their legal proceedings but nevertheless have an impact on how they conduct their day-to-day lives. Separating from your partner is an incredibly emotional time and having the right support in place will help you both adjust to your new situation.

Family consultants are experienced counsellors, coaches or mediators who work with individuals, couples and their families to help them negotiate their way through divorce, separation or some other family dispute. The aim is that you will feel empowered with support to make the difficult decisions needed.

Whilst your lawyer may be very happy to act as a sounding board for your issues they are not trained to provide answers for how you deal with your emotional issue. From a personal perspective we have found that encouraging clients to meet with a family counsellor to sort 'the emotional stuff' has meant that their legal case runs more efficiently. Efficiency = lower legal costs. Have a re-read of Jane's introduction to this book for a family consultant's view and look at her website for further information..

For some people the idea of a family counsellor is too much of an 'American' invention. Often in the States a lawyer will have a family counsellor sit in on the first meeting with a new client and they represent their clients as a 'double-act'. We have not quite progressed to that point yet but some practitioners, (particularly in East Anglia where Elisabeth is based and where Dispute Resolution is perhaps at it's greatest saturation), it is not unusual to regularly include family counsellors as a key part of the overall approach. Also remember that you may find that a family counsellor is needed a lot when you first separate but then you feel that you are back on an even keel. Don't be surprised towards the end of the legal proceedings if you feel you need some more help and support at that point.

Estate Agents/Surveyors

Often we think Estate Agents get a bad press but if you separate from your partner they play an important role when looking at a financial settlement. Invariably, there is a house to be sold or transferred from one person to the other. A valuation is going to be required before any figures can be agreed. You may be happy to accept 3 written valuations from local estate agents. This is by far the most cost-effective option.

Sometimes the property value cannot be agreed or there may be complicated issues associated with establishing a value such as a property being linked to a business whether it is a riding stables next to the family home or a family farm. Or sometimes perhaps your ex is just set in their view about how much the property is worth and without an expert's report there is no shifting them from their opinion. Maybe you find your property is going to be affected by a new road building scheme. All of these are issues that can impact on the value of a property.

When you cannot agree how much a property is worth you are going to need a formal valuation and at that point an Estate Agent is not able to provide the level of detail that will be required. This is where a Surveyor takes over. A surveyor's role is to consider firstly what the property is worth and provide evidence about why that conclusion is reached with examples of similar properties that have sold in the local area.

A Surveyor will also address any issues of difficulty. For example, what if you would like to sell the family home so you can both downsize and buy alternative housing but there is a restriction which links that property to the business on adjoining land that one of you would like to continue to run? How does this affect the value? What if you have planning permission to expand your

56

home but you have separated before doing so? If court proceedings take place a Surveyor is able to attend court and explain to a Judge why in their professional opinion a property is worth as much as they have stated in their report. An Estate Agent will not do this for you. The other practical task that you can ask your Estate Agent to help you with is to research your alternative housing options. If you have specific requirements (both in terms of budget and location) they will be able to help you narrow your search.

General Practitioner

Your GP is often the first person you confide in that you are struggling to cope with the emotional side of a relationship breakdown. With luck, you are met with a positive and supportive response. We have witnessed many clients fail to cope with the shock that a relationship is ending. It is often the response of their GP that is instrumental in how long it takes for that person to come up for air. Prescribing anti-depressants may be part of the solution, at least in the short-term, but a supportive GP who offers follow up appointments and thinks 'outside the box' rather than just prescribing medication will often make the difference. Many GP's are able to refer their patients for counselling and even if your relationship cannot be 'fixed' the counselling should help you work out what you want to achieve and assist you to be able to communicate better with your ex. GP's might be able to liase with your child's school to arrange counselling for them if required. GP's help by ensuring both parents are kept informed if you have a child who regularly requires medical treatments thus making sure the other parent who does not attend with your child at the surgery receives a letter confirming the treatment that has taken place. Very often, the act of your GP ensuring that the other parent is kept informed will ensure that arguments are stopped before they start. Prior to your separation the discussions of what happened at the GPs would have taken place at home, but if you are separated or finding it difficult to communicate this action by your GP can be incredibly helpful.

From time to time we, as lawyers, have clients who struggle to cope with the emotional impact of a relationship breakdown. Their ability to provide clear instructions to the lawyer becomes impaired. If your GP is proactive and willing to liaise with your lawyer to potentially appoint someone else to make decisions whilst you are unable to do so it saves time and money. If you have a friend or family member who you think perhaps should not be making decisions about their legal issues get them to discuss this with their GP. If your ex thinks that you are not coping and able to make decisions, or vice versa, the court can be asked to appoint someone to officially make decisions on your behalf.

Accountants/tax specialist

Not every case requires the involvement of an accountant or tax specialist. As with family counsellors, your lawyer should be able to identify when outside help is required and refer you to that specialist as soon as possible. If you run your own business or perhaps your former partner has complicated business dealings the involvement of their business accountant may be required to explain how the money within the business works and whether it is possible to borrow against the business to fund your new lives.

If you are suspicious that your former partner is not disclosing all that they should be within your financial negotiations, you may be asked to consider appointing a forensic accountant. A forensic accountant specialises in analysing, interpreting and summarising complicated financial and business related issued in a way that is understandable and properly supported with evidence. In much the same way that Actuaries are considered the 'number geeks', forensic accountants are the 'number crunchers'!

Your lawyer will not be qualified to advise you about the complicated nature of someone's business accounts, but they should be able to spot when outside help is required. If you think your lawyer is getting out of their depth or you don't fully understand the explanations you are being given ask them for an expert to be appointed to clarify the situation. Some forensic accountants work as 'shadow experts' meaning that they work alongside your lawyer and review the financial disclosure to enable your lawyer to ask questions about things that look a bit odd. Your lawyer will know forensic accountants who can help with this and we have found that this often tips the balance where there is an ex-partner who is being a bit difficult about providing information relating to their business or bank accounts.

How to get the most from your lawyer and keep your costs down

Ask any client who comes for a first meeting with their lawyer and their priorities will be to obtain the best advice for their particular situation without paying excessive legal bills. Listed below are some practical ways that you can ensure you keep your legal costs under control and at the same time get the most from the lawyer you instruct.

- Before your first meeting make a note of the key points you want to discuss and give the note to your lawyer at the start of your meeting, or better still, email it to them beforehand.

- Talk on the phone to your lawyer instead of sending numerous emails back and forth. You can cover more in a 10-minute phone call than in 6 emails back and forth!

- Try to avoid using your lawyer to provide emotional support. Lawyers are good but expensive listeners. Use your lawyers to provide the legal advice and obtain emotional support from a family counsellor.

- Be organised. Take a pen and note pad to your meeting. If your lawyer tells you to obtain a list of documents get them to your lawyer ASAP. Take someone with you to make notes for you if you think it will help. Your lawyer won't mind you bringing someone with you for additional support. Every time they chase you for some outstanding information you will be charged!

- Keep all of your documents regarding your case in a file so that you have them in one place. By the end of your case you may have received lots of correspondence and often re-reading the past few letters sent between all involved prior to a meeting will refresh your memory and perhaps answer some of the questions you have. Even better, if you are able to provide them in pdf format you will be very popular with your lawyer.

- Ask upfront what you can do yourself and which bits you need your lawyer to do. If you are confident at form-filling perhaps you could do the paperwork associated with applying for the divorce and ask your lawyer to concentrate on reaching a financial agreement. This could save you a significant sum!

- Be clear at the beginning what your legal costs budget is and apportion your money accordingly. If you are paying your lawyer on a fixed fee basis, ask if you can pay the fixed fee in bite-size portions to ease your cash flow. Don't instruct expensive experts if you cannot afford them! If experts are required make sure you agree with your former partner how they are going to be paid.

- Ask your lawyer where junior members of their team can help. Usually lawyers will have more junior members of staff and trainees who charge less per hour but will be fully able to prepare straightforward court documents. Often a trainee is half the cost of your lawyer.

- Do you need to instruct the Partner in charge of the family team who will be the most expensive?

- If you have to attend Court discuss with your lawyer whether it is more cost effective for a barrister to attend with you. Factor in the time your lawyer will spend waiting with you at court against a fixed fee that can be agreed for a barrister to attend with you. Remember that your lawyer will have good relationships with barristers' chambers and if money is short don't be too embarrassed to ask your lawyer to see if the barristers have any wriggle room.. Often they will!
- Utilise your lawyer's assistant/secretary. They work closely alongside your lawyer and if you have a straightforward question more often than not they will be able to answer it for you. You will probably find that there is no charge for this whereas if you speak to your lawyer you will be charged!
- When providing documents to your lawyer for financial disclosure ask how many copies they will need. Some law firms charge you for photocopying and this can be a hidden cost until you see your monthly invoice.
- Ask your lawyers what fixed fees they offer and what online packages are available. It is now very easy to apply online for a divorce, for example, and you might want to do this bit of the process yourself to mitigate costs.
- Ask your lawyer what other charges will be incurred. Will your lawyer obtain documents from the Land Registry as a matter of routine to establish ownership of your family home, or do they liaise with their property colleagues who may be instructed to sell your home and get copies from them?

Start thinking about the future – take a structured approach

Deciding what you want from your new life is not easy Some elements may be fairly obvious in that you may want to remain living in the same area where your children are at school or you have family and friends nearby to provide support. Other issues may not be immediately clear as you might prefer to stay living at the family home but finances prevent that from happening. However difficult it is to face unhappy truths, such as you cannot afford a mortgage the size of your current one, the earlier you accept those issues the easier it will be for you to focus on your future.

Every case is different and no two outcomes are ever the same. It used to be that the bane of a family lawyer's life was the 'advice down the pub' that their client received. More commonly now it is the information they have seen online and invariably on social media that is going to colour a person's view of the outcome they expect. Managing your expectations should be handled sensitively. If what you are seeking to achieve is not possible you should be told this as soon as possible to avoid wasted time and avoid disappointments

Listed below are some things for you to think about. Some answers will be easy but others will take time for you to come to a considered decision.

- Where would you like to live? Would you prefer to remain living in the family home or is it more practical to relocate or downsize?

- If you are going to move, what alternative housing do you need? Draw up a list of things that you 'need' such as staying within your child's current school catchment area, and things that are 'preferred', such as off road parking or a sizeable garden.
- Is renting a more practical short-term option if it means you can sell the family home and reduce your debts?
- Could you move to a Shared Ownership property so that you buy a certain percentage of the property and rent the remainder from the Housing Association?
- Will work change if you are separating? Do you need to change your working pattern to accommodate your children where before you and your former partner shared the pre and after school care? Can family members or friends help out with the practical arrangements in the short and longer term?
- What outside help do you need? If you are not financially aware is it worth meeting with an IFA to have your current financial situation clarified so you can make informed decision? Get 'money-smart'.
- What about your long-term financial security? Providing housing now and an income to meet your day-to-day needs is important but so is provision for your retirement. Does this need to be addressed as part of your overall discussions or do you both agree you are relatively young and able to make provision for yourselves?
- Have you made a new Will? What happens if either of you died before a final agreement is reached, would you want your former partner to inherit? If not, make a new Will!

- Do you need to close joint bank accounts? If one of you is moving out of the family home and moving into rented housing whilst you sort out the long-term arrangements it will probably be easier to close all joint accounts so that one of you is not concerned about the other potentially going overdrawn.

- Does one of you need interim maintenance? Are the day-to day expenses going to be met from individual income or is there a shortfall? Prioritise the bills that need paying and consider those expenses which can be cut for the time being.

- If you are both going to stay living in the family home until it is sold consider the practical arrangements. How will you feel if your former partner brings a new partner to the house? What are you going to do about the household chores? Are you going to agree who does the cooking, cleaning etc. or are you going to employ a cleaner instead?

- What arrangements need to be put in place to provide security for your children? How often will they see each parent? Do the children need emotional support from outside the family home?

- Have you made sure you have applied for any state benefits that you may qualify for? Ask the CAB to help with an initial assessment.

This is by no means an exhaustive list and just a starting point. The ideal is that you and your former partner can agree together how you will resolve your differences and how you will manage your separation. Not all couples are able to do so without the involvement of lawyers and perhaps other professionals. Just because you are pragmatic and approach matters in the most sensible way possible, there is no guarantee that your former partner will do so and for some cases court hearings and costly litigation will be inevitable.

Having advised many clients over the years our suggestion is that you look at the 'preparation questions' in the Appendix and try to answer them as honestly as you can. Ask your former partner to do the same. At its worst you will identify areas that you disagree but at its best you will be able to focus on the same goals. A frequently chosen goal among clients is the idea that when your children marry or graduate you would like to be able to both be there to support them. How you manage your divorce and the emotions that form part of that separation will be a huge factor that determines whether that is possible.

You will have probably attended many social events where friends have only been able to invite one parent for fear that if both parents are present there will be an 'atmosphere'. Is this what you want for your children? Probably not! Have that as your goal when everything seems to be too much to cope with and you won't go too far wrong in our opinion.

Now read the main points from Chapter 5 overleaf.

****

Main Points from Chapter 5

Who the Professionals Are and What They Do

➢ There are a number of professionals involved when going through a divorce, you will need to consider carefully which ones you are likely to need.

➢ A lawyer will usually be the first port of call and a good lawyer will identify early on where the professionals will be needed.

➢ Be clear at the outset what your lawyer covers in their costs and what is not included.

➢ Many family lawyers are members of Resolution and you can search their website for lawyers in your location.

➢ Start thinking now about what will happen in the future. Don't leave it until it gets messy and complicated.

****

Chapter 6

Dispute Resolution

Dispute resolution (or ADR "alternative dispute resolution" as it is often called) is a process whereby you and your ex work through your case with the aim of arriving at solutions everyone can live with. A detailed settlement can be incorporated into a Court Order if appropriate. There are a number of potential benefits for you and your family if you can settle matters between you using one of the dispute resolution processes:-

- You can maintain civil working relationships by taking your issues out of the adversarial court arena. If you are parents you will see each other for years to come, so far better for yourselves and the children if you can work together to ensure those relationships are not yet destroyed.

- You remain in control of the decisions. If you go to Court you are effectively saying to the Judge "we can't agree, so you decide'

   That is precisely what the Judge will do. Their decision may not be what either of you want. An arbitrator will also make the decisions for you.

- Time saving. You can expect the Court process to take months. With dispute resolution you are part of managing the timescale. Flexibility. It is far easier to rearrange an appointment with a mediator than a Court Hearing (although we would not encourage frequent changes as that can be indicative of a lack of commitment to participate in the process). You can ask for a break in the session.
- Costs savings. Dispute resolution is a considerably cheaper option than either negotiating through lawyers and/or going to court.
- Incorporating Additional Support. Dispute resolution processes can utilise, where necessary, referrals to other professions such as Financial Advisors, Actuaries and Counsellors.
- You can choose the process you feel is best suited to you and your needs. You both have to agree to attend for mediation or arbitration or collaborative law appointments, so that mutual choice and selection process helps to set the scene in a positive light to allow matters to proceed.

Mediation or Collaborative Law?

Mediation involves commonly a single mediator, although sometimes two mediators will work together. This is known as co – mediation. Collaborative law involves a series of round-the-table meetings between you and your ex with both lawyers present.

Mediation

Usually, a series of meetings take place between you and your ex and a mediator. The mediator's job is to put a structure to your discussions, to remain neutral, and to help you arrive at a set of proposals you can both live with. You will find that negotiations relating to both children and finances will be conducted parallel to each other, so you can expect to address both areas during each session. Sessions commonly last for about 1-1 ½ hours.

Three mediation sessions is about average, but there are no rules as to how many sessions are required. That is down to you and your mediator.

Expect to have "homework", particularly in relation to financial information. Your mediator is likely to ask you to collate details of your current financial position and to consider issues such as where you propose to live in the future.

You will need to look at the affordability of your proposals. Sometimes it can be worth considering various options if only to rule some out as being unfeasible.

You have the scope to test out some proposals, say, the children's arrangements. If a particular element doesn't work you are free to discuss it again during the next session.

Dispute Resolution involves a series of "steps". You may need to "tweak" your initial suggestions. There is absolutely nothing wrong with this – far better to resolve the problem at an early stage when you have professional support from your mediator and/or lawyer. You usually retain the services of your own lawyer throughout mediation. Indeed, mediators regularly encourage those in mediation to take their own legal advice at various stages.

A mediator cannot advise the participants in mediation. Occasionally a mediation session will take place with both lawyers present, but only if necessary as paying the costs of three professionals can provide expensive!

At the end of mediation a summary of your proposals is incorporated into what is known as a "Memorandum of Understanding". In England and Wales this document is not legally binding in itself. However it is usually incorporated into a Court Order drafted by the lawyers which can be sent for a Judge's approval without your having to turn up at Court.

If you are mediating in respect of property and financial issues you will receive another document known as an open financial statement. This is a factual summary of your financial position as a couple and it is not legally privileged, so can be seen within the court arena.

Collaborative Law

The collaborative process is very similar to mediation in that the aim is to assist you to resolve issues arising from your separation in a dignified and respectful way for the benefit of the whole family. It is a slightly different process to mediation. You and your partner retain separate, specially trained lawyers, who will assist you to resolve issues without going to court.

- Your collaborative lawyer will provide you with the advice required but will also work with your partner and their lawyer as part of a team to help reach an agreed settlement.

- You, your partner, and your lawyers agree to work together in a respectful, honest and dignified way without threatening to go to court.

- You sign an agreement disqualifying your collaborative lawyer from representing you at court if the process breaks down. Neither of the lawyers, or their respective firms, can represent you.

- Issues are discussed and hopefully resolved in a series of 'four-way' face-to-face meetings between you, your lawyer, your partner and their lawyer. Settlement discussions take place in your presence which helps to ensure that you and your partner remain in charge of the process. This process helps communication and is particularly important when you have children.

How is mediation different to Collaborative law?

- In mediation, the mediator is prohibited from giving you legal advice, and cannot assist you in advocating a position. The mediator remains neutral.

- A mediator has a duty to advise you both to take separate legal advice. This is not necessary in collaborative law as your lawyer is present with you at any discussion.
- Any settlement discussed at mediation is only binding upon you once you have each had the opportunity to take your own legal advice and have transferred the agreement into an order of the court.
- Provided it is agreed, your collaborative lawyer can act for you in the divorce and prepare the court papers to obtain the consent order.
- Although it is feasible, lawyers are rarely present during the mediation sessions, and their advice is usually obtained after a decision or order. With collaborative law you receive the legal advice at the time the issue is raised.

Round Table discussions

This is where you and your ex arrange to meet with both of your lawyers present to discuss your case. Meetings work very much like in collaborative law but the difference is that there is no requirement to sign a 'participation agreement'. The idea of 4-way meetings is gaining in popularity and we are finding that clients much prefer two or three face to face meetings to agree how they resolve their financial issues and how they will parent their children in place of 6 months of correspondence being traded between lawyers. It is a far more transparent way of working and, for lawyers, when it works well and the clients reach an agreement it is very satisfying to see an agreement come together quickly and amicably.

Family Arbitration (or pick your own Judge!)

Arbitration is another form of dispute resolution developed to deal with financial and property and children issues and is relatively new to family law (it has been a method utilised to resolve commercial and contract disputes for some time). The parties enter into an agreement whereby they appoint a qualified arbitrator to adjudicate their dispute and produce a binding result. The arbitrator effectively acts as a private judge and it is an option for couples who want to resolve financial disputes quickly without a court hearing.

Arbitration cannot be used where one party is bankrupt or insolvent. In most cases there will be a preliminary meeting and a Final Hearing if matters cannot be agreed, but arbitration can be conducted in its entirety as a paper exercise. A final decision made by an Arbitrator is known as an award. It is also possible for there to be arbitration 'on the papers only' where each lawyer sets out your position and then the arbitrator provides a written decision. Arbitration is now also available for child-related cases too.

There are a number of advantages when comparing arbitration to the Court process in that the parties can choose their arbitrator; the timeline is decided by the participants; the entire process is confidential and it is likely there will be a substantial saving of costs when compared to expensive court proceedings. Arbitration was already gaining ground but with the impact of Covid-19 and the delays that we have seen with the court system the use of Arbitration is becoming more widespread. Details can be found on the resolution website. For more information generally, see www.ifla.org.uk -Institute of Family Law arbitrators.

Summary of the respective purposes of mediation, collaborative law, arbitration and the courts.

	Mediation	Collaborative law	Arbitration	Court
Can give legal advice	NO	YES	NO	NO
Can make legally binding decisions	NO	NO	YES	YES
Legal aid available	YES	NO	NO	NO
You make the decisions	YES	YES	NO Unless you settle first	NO Unless you settle first

Now read the main points from Chapter 6 overleaf.

****

Main Points from Chapter 6

Dispute Resolution

➢ Dispute Resolution (ADR) is a process whereby you and your ex works through your case with the help of a mediator or a collaborative lawyer.

➢ The main aim of dispute resolution is to come up with solutions everyone can live with and draw up a detailed settlement.

➢ Each process is distinct from the others. In mediation, the mediator is prohibited from giving legal advice whereas this isn't the case where lawyers are involved.

➢ Family arbitration is an alternative to the court process. An arbitrator makes the decisions for you, in the same way as a Judge would.

****

Chapter 7

When to Spend Money on Professional Help

What can you do yourself?

Form-filling and online options

It used to be considered the norm that when your relationship broke down you made an appointment to meet with a solicitor and instructed them to 'sort' the issues. By that we mean apply to the court for your divorce (liaising with your former partner beforehand on the best way to achieve that) and then negotiate either directly with your former partner or their solicitor to agree the financial arrangements and practical arrangements for your children. Technology combined with the need for families to reign in their outgoings when the cost of everything around them is increasing has meant that this is no longer the norm.

In 2001 when we first qualified it was unusual for clients to be dealing directly with the court filling out their own paperwork to apply for a divorce. Public funding was freely available to assist with the cost of the divorce process and if you were paying privately it was considered the norm for your lawyer to deal with this for you. The proliferation of the internet coupled with the drastic reduction in available public funding has lead to a massive change in this process over the past 15 years.

There is a myriad of information available telling you how to apply for a divorce, together with online examples of how the forms should be completed. There are forums to discuss the best way to proceed with your case and even the Court Service have grasped the importance of modern technology and made their website fairly user-friendly. (Google 'HMCTS' and you will find all of the forms and user guides available to download).

With court fees to obtain a divorce now at £550 (current as of 2020) it is easy to see why clients don't then want to spend a further £800 inc VAT paying for their lawyer to complete forms that they feel able to do themselves. Some law firms offer fixed-fee divorces.

The benefit of both of this to you as the client is that you keep your costs under control. Nationwide there has been a huge increase in lawyers using the online divorce system and every family lawyer has been encouraged to sign up.

We can confirm the system, when it works smoothly, is amazing! There are a few glitches along the way and the odd time that we login an find the system is down is annoying but overall the speed and ease with which we as lawyers are now able to apply for a divorce, or ask the court to approve a financial agreement is a game-changer. The regional divorce units that were introduced to supposedly speed up the process just weren't able to keep pace with demand.

What if your case has complicated elements?

The difficulty for both of the above options is that they will not be appropriate if your case is anything other than straightforward. By that we mean you do not know where your former partner is living outside of England and Wales, or perhaps they contest the divorce application making it a more complicated process than normal. If your divorce has an element of complication you would be wise to ask your lawyer to deal with the process for you. Otherwise you may find yourself unable to progress the divorce as quickly as possible. Talk to your lawyer at the outset and ask them to assess whether your case is one which they should deal with or one that you can process the paperwork yourself. If you do want to do most of the work yourself talk to your lawyer about them acting for you on an ad hoc basis to check the paperwork as you go through the process. Be clear with them about what you expect them to do so that you don't receive an invoice out of the blue.

How much can you DIY when it comes to agreeing the children's arrangements?

It is not just divorce applications where clients are tending to take the lead. The concept of 'shared care' arrangements for children is far more common than it was 15 years ago. The reality is that the courts only make a handful of court orders confirming the care arrangements that are already in place. Many parents agree plans between themselves without ever involving the courts or even their lawyers in the negotiations. It is agreed

79

when they separate where the children will live and how the day-to-day arrangements will work.

If you and your ex want to reach an agreement about how you parent your children but find it is too difficult to talk about think about asking a family consultant to help you work out the arrangements. They will charge you less than a lawyer and you will probably also find that you communicate better with each other in the long term.

Even for those cases where parents are unable to reach an agreement before instructing solicitors, the way that the court process is structured encourages negotiation between you as parents rather than the Judges determining the final arrangements. Of course, if you are unable to reach an agreement ultimately the court will make a decision locally. The judiciary are telling us lawyers that Mediation helps to reduce their workload as many cases can be resolved without the court having to make decisions on behalf of the parents. How much of this is motivated by parents looking to save costs versus the systemic changes that have been implemented is difficult to identify but the end result is that we as lawyers are seeing less contested children related cases than ever before.

The downside of public funding no longer being available is that for those parents who are not able to agree how they will co-parent their children, court applications follow and invariably the Judges are telling us that those parents are acting without legal advice (litigants in Person or LP's).

We know from firsthand experience that the number of people who attend court without legal advice is increasing leading to a higher work load for the court. If you want to go to court and do not want to instruct a lawyer, think about having a first meeting with a lawyer so that you know the process and can ensure that you make the correct application and are aware of what will happen when you attend court.

Preparation is the key if you are acting without a lawyer! There are some pro bono (free) services available and the Anglia Ruskin Law family law clinic is an excellent example of where local lawyers and law students work together to help some people in need. However, this can't reach everyone that needs help.

What about the financial issues too?

If you are trying to resolve financial issues the DIY approach is not beyond you either. It really depends on how confident you are in firstly dealing with the assets and liabilities that you have and secondly whether you believe that your former partner is being honest with you about what assets and liabilities that you have. Sitting down together at the kitchen table and agreeing 'who has what' has always happened but there has been a real increase in people trying to reach an agreement with minimal involvement of their lawyers in the past 15 years. If you can generate a simple Excel spreadsheet setting out the assets and liabilities that would help you too.

The end result for us as lawyers is that we tend to deal with far more people who have an agreement in place and want us to prepare the necessary paperwork prepared for the court to approve the settlement than ever before. From time to time lawyers may question the settlement that you have agreed if it appears a bit too one-sided or perhaps there are issues that have been overlooked. However, it is always pleasing to deal with a couple who have made a decision about how their financial issues will be agreed without the need for litigation. The biggest motivating force for couples to reach agreements is the drive to save costs.

What does this mean for your lawyer in terms of their role?

Firstly, your lawyer is still the main point of reference for all legal advice but the difference to their role compared to say 15 years ago is the fact that they will be dealing with far more clients who are compartmentalising their cases. The lawyers may be charged with sorting out the financial side of things but the clients are agreeing between themselves either with or without the assistance of a third party the arrangements for the children. The client will more likely apply for the divorce 'in person' and referring to their lawyer for advice if they are uncertain how to complete a specific part of the application process.

It is now mandatory for all people to have a mediation referral before making an application to the court for anything other than divorce. There are exceptions where it is not appropriate for a couple to mediate but that change means that all lawyers now routinely deal with mediators. There will remain some individuals for whom a referral to mediation is simply a 'hoop' that a client jumps through before they issue their application at court. However, there are also more cases where clients see the benefits of mediation and use that as a method to resolve their disputes rather than have letters being traded between solicitors or an application being made to the court.

Anecdotal evidence from the judiciary suggests that the number of cases being issued in court reduced after the mediation requirement was introduced. It is also true that of those people who make applications to the court, like with children related cases, far more are now made by people who do not have lawyers. This created a different challenge for the court system as Litigants in Person are not lawyers, so at times the judiciary must explain in more detail what is expected from them at each individual hearing. Inevitably, it also means there are more and more court documents completed with errors and being bounced back by the admin team.

How do you approach DIY?-Identify your strengths

Before you commit to take on responsibility for some or all aspects of your divorce, finances, or children related disputes identify your strengths. Are you comfortable form-filling or is it the last thing you want to spend your evenings doing? Are you organised? If not, you need to be clear on the time scales for completing various forms before you fall foul of the court system. If you want to take on the task of your own divorce or children dispute proceedings, make sure you write down all the dates by when forms must be completed. Get a diary!

Get organised

Make sure that you have plenty of blank copies to fill in before-hand so that you can present a clear copy to the court and if your handwriting is shocking, use one of the online packages so that you can have the form typed, or ask a friend who has better writing than you. Don't be tempted to do as the doctors do on your prescriptions! If the writing on your forms is not clear it will cost you time in delays and misunderstandings. If you are dealing with financial issues, make sure you have copies of all documents you are sending to your former partner's lawyers or to other third parties such as mediators or financial advisors. Keep a careful note of what needs to go where and when so that you are not buried in requests for paperwork.

Be systematic about looking through any documents sent to you. Are there any questions that you have arising out of that disclosure? If so, ask them sooner rather than later. Do you need to involve a specialist to prepare a report if you are talking about complicated financial issues such as pensions or life insurance cover. Do you fully understand how the various investments work?

What additional help do you need?
Would it be sensible to ask a financial advisor to review your financial documents and answer any questions at an early stage?

It may be that worries you have about, say, affordability of mortgages if you both sold the family home and purchased two separate houses are unfounded. Do you need to investigate the tax consequences if it is not possible for one of you to take on responsibility for the mortgage so instead the mortgage and family house remains in joint names for the time being but one of you moves out? When you sell the house in the future what Capital Gains Tax will need to be paid and how will that get factored into any agreement you have?

Are pensions going to be an issue? Do you need an Actuary to prepare a report to look at all the options available to you? If one of you works in the public sector and one of you in the private sector your pension provision could be vastly different, particularly if one of you still has a 'final salary' based pension. An actuarial report will cost money but if it presents the options to you clearly and you are then able to agree what percentage of a particular pension is transferred to the other person to provide a fair retirement income, is it money well spent?

Be realistic

Be realistic about what can be achieved if you and your former partner go to mediation. It is not the panacea to solve all problems. The good thing about mediation is that it encourages better communication between you, which is particularly helpful if you have children and therefore continue to co-parent. However, if one of you is not a good listener and still feels very angry then it will not be a great success! Maybe it is wiser to take things slower at the outset to allow the person who did not see the end of your relationship coming time to adjust?

Think about whether it is a cost-effective option to involve a Family Consultant. Is one of you more emotionally vulnerable than the other. Would the overall process work better if the more vulnerable one of you had support? It is often said that separating from your partner is akin to bereavement. Having witnessed countless numbers of people dealing with their separation it is easy to see why this is true. As a family lawyer you get used to having a constant supply of tissues to hand. The level of anger or emotional vulnerability changes from case to case but mostly it takes the person finding out that their relationship is ending at least 6 months to adjust to that concept.

Remember this is an emotional process

Often one of you will have been thinking about separating for a while before mentioning it to the other. The way that information is processed hugely affects how your case progresses. For some, there is a general acceptance that the relationship has run its course. For others there is also anger that the relationship is ending and not what they want. There is also shock that it is happening and fears about where they will live and how they will cope with the change to both their lives and their children's lives.

In a way, it is easier to deal with those people who react angrily at first as often, given enough time and space they will calm down. Sometimes, the early involvement of a family counsellor is helpful to as it enables those people who do feel angry and fearful for their future to have an outlet for those emotions and develop a strategy to move forwards. The expansion in the number of family counsellors available has, in part, been led by the move towards Collaborative law. One of the positives to the collaborative process which was led by a few practitioners in East Anglia is that we as lawyers communicate better with each other. We are more minded to involve family counsellors etc. as we have seen how they interact with our clients firsthand. It is far easier to sell a concept to someone when you, as their lawyer, understand how it works and what the benefits to that person are going to be. In the Cambridge area, for example, the lawyers, family consultants and IFA's regularly get together to train and socialise.

Make a list of those things you disagree about

If possible, try to agree what you disagree on. That might sound like a bizarre comment to make but at least if you are agreed on say two thirds of the issues following your separation it means that you can instruct your lawyers to determine those outstanding issues only. This in itself saves time and costs.

If, for example, you are both agreed that the family home is to be sold, the mortgage repaid, and the equity divided in specific percentages but you cannot agree what will happen in terms of pension provision then you can ask your lawyers to advise you on the options. Of course you will pay for their time and expertise, and also possibly an Actuarial report if you want to transfer part of one pension fund to the other person, but you are far better to do that than say everything is 'off the table' and you start again.

When you have issues upon which you are agreed acknowledge that and make the money that you do have available to spend on lawyers work to your advantage! Much as you wouldn't necessarily employ a landscape gardener to mow your grass but you would to terrace a steep garden, use your lawyers and other professionals where you need expert help. Do the simple tasks yourself if you can!

Be honest with your lawyer about your budget to pay them and anyone else

Don't be afraid of saying to your lawyer upfront that you have a budget of £x and you need to agree at the start where it is best to spend that money to get you the best outcome possible. An IFA can explain whether or not you need to keep various policies running or whether it would be better to cash them in now. Mediators, if used, may charge less per hour than the lawyers to resolve disputes between you and your former partner.

If you are asking various third parties to get involved, make sure your lawyer keeps a tight check on the expenses involved and agree with your former partner who is going to pay for which third party expense. Will they be shared equally or are you intending to use a particular 'pot' of money to pay for that expense? If you already have an IFA involved and you then ask an Actuary to prepare a report make sure that they speak to each other. Often there will be a cross-over in the information they both need and by ensuring they both share information you may find the reports are prepared faster and answer the specific concerns you both have to better effect.

Where you are asking experts to prepare reports make sure your lawyer has a signed 'letter of authority' from you so that your Actuary, IFA etc. can contact the necessary organisations such as each individual pension company to obtain up to date valuations. Not only will this save time but it means they can get the information that they want to complete the task they have been set rather than the information you believe they want which is not always the same thing!

So what bits is it best not to DIY?

As with many things there are some bits that are best left to the professionals. If money is tight and you can reach an agreement about finances between yourselves don't be tempted to think that you don't need to use a lawyer at all. You can apply for the divorce yourself, and you can reach an agreement yourself too but the court will require a properly drafted document to confirm the financial settlement which needs to be prepared by a lawyer. If you do not have a court approved financial agreement you leave yourself open to further financial argument later.

Most separating couples aim to have a 'clean break' meaning that they divide their assets and liabilities upon separation and after that they go their separate ways. They may have an agreement in place for how they support their children but the arrangements in place for the adults are final. This can only happen if the court approves a Consent Order. (A financial agreement drafted by lawyers and signed by both people involved which confirms that a deal is agreed).

Whilst you will have to pay for a lawyer to prepare this document, even if you do everything else yourself it is still money well spent. If everything is agreed it should not take your lawyer more than 3 or 4 hours for a straightforward deal to be put into writing, signed by both people involved and sealed by the court. The knowledge that your deal is 'watertight' is, in our opinion, worth paying for. This is where you should prioritise your spending.

Now read the main points from Chapter 7 overleaf.

****

Main Points from Chapter 7

When to Spend Money on Professional Help

➤ With the advent of the internet, the proliferation of information concerning divorce and the steps taken to commence divorce, it is now usual for those seeking divorce to take a number of actions themselves before incurring costs.

➤ The more complicated your circumstances, the more you will need the help of lawyers in the early stages.

➤ Many partners will agree among themselves child care and sharing arrangements without involving lawyers. This too saves time and money.

➤ If you are trying to resolve financial issues, the DIY approach is not beyond you. However, this will depend on your level of confidence and co-operation with your partner.

➤ Your lawyer is still your main point of reference for all legal advice, rather than "barrack room" lawyers. However, it is true to say that much more can be achieved yourself, thereby saving money.

➤ Make sure you have a Consent Order even if you negotiate the financial details directly with your ex.

Chapter 8

Children

How you sort out your children's arrangements now sets the footing for the future of the whole family.

Do your homework, communicate with clarity, avoid ambiguity and be prepared to be flexible. You then have a head start to making arrangements for your children work. Parents play a major role in promoting children's long-term adjustment to family change. Parents can protect children from the stress and anguish of separation by providing nurturing supportive and dependable relationships.

You may not be able to prevent your children from being upset, but you can support them and help them to adjust to and cope with major change in their lives.

Build good relationships with your children by spending time alone with them, being interested in their lives and activities, and showing them empathy and respect. Reassure your children about the future, and reinforce the fact that the separation was not their fault. Look after yourself – you have to care for them so you need to be up to the job! Communicate openly with your children. This doesn't mean providing them with all the lurid details, but be honest and open with them. Listen to them and try to put yourself in their place. Be available to them and encourage them to talk. Remember though that they are children and not adults.

Try to manage the amount of change in their lives at any one time. If you can, make change gradual and give children time to prepare for it. Keep it positive when discussing change with the children and try to give them time to get used to things.

Create a stable home environment. Have organised routines, clear rules and boundaries. Resolve the arrangements for the children as quickly as you can and support the children in their relationship with the other parent. Whatever you do, don't use the children as pawns in a battle with the other parent.

The Effects of Children's ages
Babies – 2 years old
Under 2 years of age it is unlikely children will remember much, and they quickly settle into new routines. However, babies will pick up on tension, anxiety and arguments. Don't let them be aware of rows, give them lots of cuddles and reassurance. You will also need to bear in mind they will not grow up in a home with both parents and care must be taken to tell them why as soon as they are old enough.

Toddlers – 2 –5 years
Children in this age range understand what a fight is, they will understand some of the language used, and again they will pick up on a negative atmosphere.

They may worry because one parent has left and this often manifests itself in the child's behaviour – poor sleeping, crying are just two symptoms.

However, with plenty of love and reassurance they soon settle into a new routine. Routine is the key and if both parent's can maintain these routines children will settle. Do your best and be persistent.

Schoolchildren aged 6-11

Let the children at this age have some reassurance that they are not losing you. They will worry that if one parents leaves, the other one may leave too. Let your children's teachers know about the split so they can let you know if any problems manifest themselves at school. Don't let your usual routines and boundaries slip because you feel the need to compensate the children for the fact that you have separated from the other parent.

Teenagers

Teenagers may appear like they are not bothered, but don't be fooled – they may well still be very upset by the separation.

Give them time to talk and stay interested and involved in their lives even if they try to stay 'cool' about things. Take their views into account when sorting out the arrangements for them to spend time with each of you. Make it clear you are the parents and will make the decisions but you are dealing with young people who have valid opinions, and those views will be taken into account.

Teenagers still need affection and your support so let them know you're there for them. Also be aware that if you find that you need emotional help then most likely so will they. It might be that their school or college tutors are able to help but also think about talking to your ex and jointly arranging for your teenage children to talk to a family counsellor.

Often we find that older children find it hardest to process the fact that their parents are separating and if the family home is being sold it might be that is the only place they as teenagers have ever lived. So, in addition to the change in where they live, they are also keenly aware of how upset their parents are that they have separated.

Talking to your children

Make positive comments about the other parent. Your children aren't separating from your ex-partner. They cannot change who their parents are. Remember the subject of the other parent is going to be talked about between you and your children. Also remember that children listen to what you say about the other parent. It is so important they hear you talking nicely about the other parent.

So, find something positive to say because your children will love both parents, no matter how things have broken down between

95

you. In time, you may become grandparents and if you are not able to have a good relationship with your children then you certainly won't be seeing much of your future grandchildren in years to come.

Parental Alienation

If one parent turns a child against the other, this is often called Parental Alienation Syndrome or PAS, a term first introduced in the 1980's by child psychiatrist Dr Richard Gardner.

What is it? It is where one parent persistently puts the other parent down to the children to the point when the children reject the denigrated parent and claim it is their own decision not to see that parent.

What your children want most is to be able to freely love both parents. Avoid saying things like 'you're just like your father/mother'. Hearing negative comments like this erodes the self- love a child has from both and impacts on their self-esteem. An angry parent doesn't equate to a good parent. Children need both parents, so allow them that necessity in their life. Parents who really care about their children will endeavour to find a way to let children enjoy a relationship with the other parent without feeling caught in the middle of a battle between Mum and Dad. Ask yourself the following questions, and if you answer yes to any of them, then you should look at, and if necessary, moderate your behaviour:

•	Do I speak negatively or critically about the other parent and their family in front of the children or within their earshot?	Yes	No
•	Do I talk about legal matters, money or child support in front of the children?	Yes	No
•	Do I quiz the children about what they have done with the other parent?	Yes	No
•	Do I stop the children having phone calls, letters or gifts from the other parent ?	Yes	No
•	Do I impede the other parents' arrangements with the children by making my own which cross over or insisting mine take precedence?	Yes	No
•	Do I pressurise or encourage the children to take sides?	Yes	No
•	Do I ask the children if they love me more?	Yes	No
•	Do I let the children know I'm upset when they are with the other parent?	Yes	No
•	Do I prevent the children from expressing their feelings if I don't like what I hear?	Yes	No

Telling the children

This is something many parents will say is the hardest thing they have ever had to do. If you are not sure how to approach this talk to a family consultant, preferably with your ex, so that you have an agreed strategy.

However, once the children have been told, they will often express some relief and acceptance because they probably knew something was up anyway! Parents should always remember; the children probably know more than parents think they do. Children are also sensitive to atmospheres between parents even if they haven't witnessed an argument. The difference between a 3 year old and 13 year old is that the 13 year old will probably be able to tell you they had thought your separation was likely to happen but both will have been aware of tensions within the family home.

So, if you have made the decision to separate, get on with it and tell the children. If you can do it together, so much the better. The children can hear it from you both, you can share the burden of the difficult task, and they can ask any questions of both of you.

Telling them together will also help to reinforce the message to the children that you both will be involved in their future and that you are fully supportive of the children spending time with both of you. Make a plan. Discuss what you are going to say to the children. Keep it simple, do not apportion blame for the split and ensure you tell the children it's not their fault.
Tell the children as far as you can what is going to happen for example:

- Where you will all be living
- The arrangements for the time they spend with each of you
- Who is taking them to school (if there are any changes)?

- When they will see the extended family (e.g. grandparents)
- If you are still in the process of making decisions, then say so. Ensure you tell them you will tell them as soon as you know.

Answer their questions as far as you can but try to keep reasons for the split non-specific. For example, Mum and Dad have decided 'we don't want to live together anymore'. Rather than 'your father/mother has left me and its all their fault'.

Try not to be angry or upset in front of the children, so work out how you will deal with this first.

Give the children time subsequently to talk about their feelings and ask any questions. Don't forget, this doesn't apply only to young children. Adult children can be devastated when their parents separate. Remember, for your children it will feel destabilizing, uncertain and distressing. We all have an image of a 'perfect' family living together harmoniously but life doesn't always work out like that.

However, the children can still have security, stability, harmony and two loving and caring parents. It's just that they have two homes now instead of one,

Common questions children ask

'Why are you getting divorced?' 'Do you still love mummy/daddy?' 'Why did mummy/daddy leave?' 'If daddy/mummy lets me do it why can't you?' 'Do I have to like mummy/daddy's new partner?'

Arrangements for Children during a Pandemic or other emergency

2020 has proved to be a very challenging and difficult time for everyone, thanks to the coronavirus pandemic. Here are some tips we hope you find helpful in a fluid and sometimes frightening situation.

- Stay safe and heed government guidance and medical advice.
- Adhere to any legal changes, whether national or local.
- Plan to meet those changes. For example you may need to change a handover location if your usual location is closed.
- Make sure you communicate effectively as parents.
- Keep your children's interests uppermost.
- Don't use the situation as an opportunity to punish your ex by preventing the children from seeing the other parent. None is this is the childrens' fault.
- Make sure you both know what the arrangements are at your child's school for attendance, mask wearing, meals, participation in sport and so on.
- Cut each other some slack. You may find yourselves in a wholly unforeseen situation. Talk about it, be practical, and supportive.

- Don't forget to keep the children informed, and manage the changes together. When their routine has suffered a significant amount of disruption, talk to them and explain why without blaming the other parent.
- Try to maintain a form of routine for you and your children.
- Use you preferred provider of video call to maintain contact with the other parent and with extended family, particularly when travel is not possible, for example during a lockdown. The children can then see those people are safe and well.

Use some of the excellent books currently available to help explain things to the children. A list of suggested titles can be found in the reference section at the end of the book.

Now read the main points from Chapter 8 overleaf.

****

Main Points from Chapter 8.

Children

➢ How you sort out your children's arrangements now sets the footing for the future of the whole family.

➢ You may not be able to prevent your children from being upset, but you can support them and help them adjust and cope with major change in their life.

➢ Whatever you do, don't use the children as pawns in a battle with the other parent.

➢ When talking to your children, always try to be positive. Your children are not separating from their parents. They can't change who their parents are.

➢ Make a plan-discuss what you are going to say to the children.

➢ In an emergency such as the coronavirus pandemic, make sure that you stick to government guidelines and medical advice.

****

Chapter 9

Parenting Plans

In this chapter we have devised a form of parenting plan we hope you will find useful. Utilise as much or as little as you wish. It will help the whole family to know what arrangements are and avoid last minute arguments. Try it and see. Consider using sticker charts for the younger children in conjunction with the parenting plan. Let the children see it if they are old enough. If they are older teenagers consider including them in your discussions.

It is well worthwhile spending a little time to formulate a plan. Whilst it's an informal commitment you both make, having something in writing you have discussed and agreed can save a lot of time, energy and upset later on. You wouldn't start a business without a business plan, and a parenting plan is a similar tool.

Keep a copy in both homes and let anyone else involved such as grandparents know what your arrangements are. Don't forget it can be amended if needs be. It is not a court order but a flexible working document with the intention of bringing some clarity to busy family life.

PARENTING PLAN

WE ARE

MUM: _____

DAD: _____

CHILDREN:

NAME   DOB/AGE
SCHOOL/NURSERY/CLGE/UNI

_____ _____   _____

_____ _____   _____

_____ _____   _____

OUR PROMISE TO EACH OTHER AND TO OUR CHILDREN

We respect and trust each other as parents and we acknowledge the children's needs to enjoy a relationship with both of us.

We will both endeavour to foster and encourage these relationships.

We recognised our children's needs to feel loved by both of us. We accept the need for cooperation between ourselves when making decisions concerning the children.

This plan is intended to provide clarity and stability for each of us and the children.

Signed _____   dated _____
      Mum

Signed _____   dated _____
      Dad

EMERGENCY CONTACT DETAILS

Dad   **Mum**

Home _____   Home _____

Work _____   Work _____

Mobile _____   Mobile_____
email   email

Children's Mobile Numbers/ other relatives / Friends:

Name _____   Name _____
Home _____   Home _____

Work _____   Work _____

Mobile _____   Mobile

School/Nursery
Name
Address
Contact at the school
Phone:
email:

Grandparents/other relatives
Name

_____

Phone

_____

Clubs

_____

_____

_____

_____

GP / Hospital / Dentist / Optician

_____

_____

_____

_____

LIVING ARRANGEMENTS

You will need to work out when the children are going to be with each parent. Use the points below to formulate your plan. It can be helpful to use a calendar, and an electronic calendar you can both edit can be useful. These are widely available on the internet.

Elements to take into account when developing a Parenting Plan.

1. Work / School / Nursery

- These elements are to a large extent non-negotiable. School times and terms are set well in advance (at the beginning of each academic year) and need to be worked round.
- School holiday timetables are usually available within a couple of weeks into each new school year. Make sure you both have one.

- The same is true for parents' working arrangements. If you are employed on a shift or agency basis, try asking your employer for as much advance notice as possible of future shift patterns. Then provide the other parent with those details.

- Even if you work regular hours – i.e. the same every week, consider asking your employer if they can be flexible – for example by allowing you to finish or start early or to work

107

flexi-time. Don't forget to tell the other parent if you are able to rearrange your working arrangements.

2.   Children's Activities

These vary from after school clubs to sports/dance/drama and so on. Write out a timetable for each child as this will help you to see where the activities slot into your parenting plan.

1) Remember activities are important to the children. They will be thrilled that both parents can see what they have achieved.

2) Don't use activities as a means of impeding the other parent. If football is every Saturday morning and the children spend alternate weekends with each of you then either take it in turns to go to football or agree the same parent will do "the football run" every week.

3.   Travel

- Who is collecting and returning the children?
- What times will be set down?
- Who is paying for the travel?
- Are car seats necessary and available?
- How will your handover take place and where will it take place?

4. Holidays

- Do changes need to be made to your usual routine to cover school holidays?
- Are you both taking the children away?
- How much notice are you going to give each other when managing a booking?

CHILDRENS LIVING ARRANGEMENTS

_____
_____
_____
_____
_____
_____
_____
_____
_____
_____
_____
_____
_____

5. Special Days

For example:-

- Christmas
- Birthdays

- Mothers and Fathers Days
- Other special days for your family

All need to be considered in your plan. Sometimes it is not easy to share special days such as Christmas. Consider an alternate year-on year arrangement if it helps- for example if travel on Christmas Day is a problem.

OUR ARRANGEMENTS FOR SPECIAL DAYS

_____
_____
_____
_____
_____
_____
_____
_____
_____
_____

6. Phone calls

Do you need to include in your Plan time for phone calls between the children and each parent?

You may need to consider more formal arrangements if telephone calls have proved problematic.

It is worth considering setting a day and time for phone calls as putting a structure to the arrangements can help to avoid misunderstandings?

Remember children don't always chat for long periods so consider a text message if they are old enough to use Skype, facetime or what's app if you have it.

OUR ARRANGEMENTS FOR PHONE CALLS

_____

_____

_____

_____

_____

_____

_____

_____

_____

_____

7. House rules in each parents home

It can be ok if these are different as long as clear boundaries are in place for the children and both they and you know what they are.

Consider:-   bed times

               Meal times

               Discipline

               Pet care

Household tasks
TV's in bedrooms
Computer Access
Time allotted on social media

HOUSE RULES   HOUSE RULES
MUM   DAD

_____

_____

_____

_____

_____

_____

_____

_____

8. Financial Matters

Consider how you will cover the day-to-day costs of the children. So, who will pay for:-

Clothes – casual   **Holidays**
School uniforms   Cost of holiday
Sports equipment   Spending
Money
Shoes
Passports/Visas

School

Trips

Lunches

After school breakfast Clubs

Travel to / from school

After school care

Nursery Fees

Book and Stationery Fees

Medical

Dental Costs

Optician costs

Prescription fees

Who will manage the children's bank accounts?

OUR FINANCIAL ARRANGEMENTS FOR THE CHILDREN

_____

_____

_____

_____

_____

_____

_____

9. School / Education

- How are you both going to be involved in the children's education?
- Will you go to parents evenings / sports days / graduation ceremonies? Together?
- How will you discuss choices e.g.   which school?
  which university?
  which exam choices?

With each other, the school and your children?

- Will one of you ensure the other has a copy of the school reports?
- Who will tell the school any important changes?

OUR DECISIONS ABOUT EDUCATION

_____

_____

_____

_____

_____

_____

_____

_____

_____

_____

10. Communication

- How are you going to communicate? Do you need to set a meeting with an agenda? If so, try to set up somewhere neutral, keep it business like and keep a record of what was agreed (minutes!)
- What are you going to do in the event of an emergency?
- How will you introduce new partners to the children (and to each other)?
- How will you manage disagreements?

- Are these decisions each of you can take without consulting the other first?
- What decisions must be taken jointly?
- If the children are away – e.g. a sleepover with friends – do we always need to tell each other where they are?
- What happens if one of us dies?
- How much notice do we need to provide if we wish to change arrangements?

OUR COMMUNICATION PLAN

_____

_____

_____

_____

_____

_____

Be aware that your child's behaviour may change as a result of your separation. Some of this may be a reaction to the changes that are happening as a result of your separation. If you find that you are struggling, et help from a parenting coach. Remember that when children are born they do not come with a manual and sometimes a little extra help can go a long way! www.parentingpeople.co.uk

It can be particularly helpful to deal with difficulties you have in communicating with each other by addressing them within your plan.

So, for example, only call/text each other at work in the event of an emergency. Keep communications polite and factual and don't go over past events.

Use a book for day to day stuff which can travel with the children - e.g.

"Anna has had her medication today"
"The children's books are in their bags"

11. Managing changes

This can be fraught. You have a working routine and then one of you needs to change it and a row ensues. It happens all the time so the key is to decide how you want to approach changes to the routine.

Decide how much notice is acceptable to you both in situations like holidays, weddings, special trips or family events. If either of you can be called into work at short notice, then how do you deal with that? What about illness and health concerns. It can be helpful to establish a time- frame such as 24 or 48 hours notice as a minimum or perhaps a month to discuss a holiday.

More significant changes such as moving home, changing school, remarriage or moving in with a new partner can also be covered in your plan.

OUR TIMESCALES FOR DISCUSSION ABOUT CHANGE

_____

_____

_____

Now read the main points from Chapter 9 overleaf.

****

Main Points from Chapter 9

Parenting Plans

➢ It is very useful to put together a parenting plan. This provides a structure for the future. Keep a copy in both homes.

➢ A parenting plan is not a court order but a flexible working document with the intention of bringing some clarity to future family life.

➢ The plan can cover every element of life, including living arrangements, financial matters, school and communications generally.

➢ Consider including how you will manage changes in the future.

****

Chapter 10

Moving on

The rules early on

The decision to move forwards and establish a different type of relationship with your former partner is not easy and for some people it will continue to be a challenge many years after you have separated. They key to a successful transition from being partners to being able to communicate successfully as former partners is to try and get it right at the beginning. By that, we mean from an early stage try to avoid becoming involved in discussions that you know will end in arguments. Try to focus on the immediate needs that you each have, and your children have, rather than score points against the other person. Whilst it might feel good for the moment to 'have your say' it usually leads to further spats which more times than not severely damage the communication between separating couples.

All too often we meet people who have separated from their former partner and initially it is amicable, and they intend to resolve their issues without the need for lawyers to be involved. Some achieve their aim but many others do not. It sounds a very common-sense point to make but when couples separate one or both of them are highly likely to be hurt and angry. For some people this makes them less likely to be able to communicate effectively with their former partner. Others, especially where they are the person that has been thinking about ending the relationship for some time, are more pragmatic in their approach. Even then, it is important to acknowledge that whilst you may feel ok about your separation if your former partner is still trying to adjust, you will have to give them time and space to get used to the new situation. There will be little chance of negotiating a long-term settlement on financial issues or the arrangements for the care of your children until the dust has settled. Tempers need to calm!

How you handle yourself in the early weeks and months will go a long way towards impacting on firstly how much you spend on your lawyers, and secondly, how long your case will take to resolve. We have all heard of cases where one person is particularly vitriolic towards their former spouse leading to court hearing after court hearing taking place and the communication between them being non-existent.

As lawyers, we feel strongly that whilst there will always be couples that find themselves unable to communicate well it is imperative that we put the long-term needs of our clients first and focus on their long-term goals, such as being able to co-parent their children together, rather than scoring short-term points and 'getting one over' on the other party. A key part of this for you as the client is to feel comfortable with your chosen lawyer and, if possible, instruct a Resolution member. If a lawyer is a member of Resolution (formerly called the Solicitors Family

Law Association) it means that they subscribe to the code of conduct ensuring that all family issues are dealt with in as non-confrontational way as possible.

Quite frankly, there is little point in you and your former partner agreeing to try your best to be calm and amicable if one of you then instructs the 'pit bull' lawyer who threatens to 'shake things up'. When you instruct your lawyer meet with them and trust your gut instinct. If they are not willing to talk to you initially on the telephone before you make an appointment, consider how approachable they will be if you instruct them? Be clear about what they charge and how you will pay their bill. Also ask how accessible they are and how hands-on is their assistance.

Get help if you need it

All too often we as lawyers are faced with clients who are incredibly hurt or angry and spend a disproportionate amount of our time dealing with the emotional fall-out of a relationship breaking down. Whilst this is an inevitable part of our role as family lawyers we are not always best placed to offer the practical help that a person in this situation requires.

Sometimes it is a simple thing like getting the support from your family and friends to enable you to move forwards and think about how you are going to live without your former partner being around 24/7. There may be practical issues you need to address such as getting to grips with dealing with your own finances if the bills have been dealt with by your former partner whilst you were together. Suddenly finding that you have to renew your car insurance for the first time in 10 years can be daunting and this is by no means the most complex task you will find you have to deal with. The Martin Lewis website is particularly useful and provides lots of practical help on how to organise your finances when there are significant changes in your life such as relationship breakdowns, children being born, retirement etc.

There is a greater acceptance of employing outside help to deal with the emotional issues following a relationship breakdown. There are many practicing lawyers throughout the country who now routinely meet with their client and at the first meeting they will have a discussion with them about when to involve a family counsellor or therapist. The idea being that the lawyer deals with the legal issues and the family counsellor or therapist deals with the emotional issues. We have had first-hand experience of where this has worked successfully with clients. It can also be a more cost-effective way for a case to be run, as if a person is particularly upset and hurt the family counsellor is vitally important in those early stages. Without their support and encouragement, the client feels vulnerable. It is also pleasing to see that during the case the client, who started out being hurt, shocked and most of all sad, improves and starts to see that whilst their relationship with their former partner has changed there are positive things to look forward to. It is just that their future is going to be different to that which they had initially planned

If you have children together in our opinion it is even more important to sort the emotional issues out early rather than later on when one of you is increasingly bitter. You may be separating from your former partner but you are parents for the rest of your life. There will be events where your children would like you both to be present. If you don't handle this bit of your life correctly at the outset it will impact on you and your children for many years to come. Some clients find it helpful to focus on a long-term goal such as enabling communication to continue so that you are both able to attend your child's university graduation or wedding.

Also remember that when the dust is settling and your legal proceedings are coming to an end this is another 'crunch' point where it is not uncommon for people to feel lost and uncertain about their future. Maybe you did not feel the need to get outside help and support when you first separated but now find that you are struggling.

If you think of separating from your partner as being similar to a grief cycle the analogy isn't too far from that. What we mean is that there is lots of upset and anger at the beginning, then you adjust, then there is more upset and anger later on too. Sometimes it can be a relatively trivial thing that sets you off at the end whether that be us lawyers sending you your Decree Absolute or handing in the keys when the sale of the family home completes. This is why we have tended to opt to call our clients when the decree absolute arrives. Without fail, our clients have a reaction to the marriage ending. We have seen everything from tears to one client who shouted loudly how she was going to 'crack open the bottle of fizz she'd been saving!' Everyone is different and if your lawyer realises that, you're probably going to form a good working relationship

Don't just talk – listen too

The importance of listening to what your former partner is saying and trying to understand why they are saying it is often under-estimated. For example, why is your former partner saying that they MUST remain living in the former family home? Is what they really mean that they want to ensure that the children stay within their current school and friendship groups? Is there any way that this can be accommodated whilst also ensuring that the family home could be sold to realise two properties being purchased? Or, are they scared of making the change if that home has been the family base for the entire length of your relationship? Change is scarier for some people than others, and if that change has been foisted upon you by a change of circumstances there could be resentment.

If what your former partner is saying makes you cross remember to take a deep breath, and if needed take a day or so to respond. (We as lawyers often do this when we receive correspondence from our colleagues that make us want to shout!) Making a decision when you are angry and cross rarely goes well! Take a day to calm down and you will deal with the issue far better. Don't suddenly announce to your former partner that a major change is going to happen, for example, the money you give them each month is suddenly going to be reduced by 50%. Think ahead to what the reaction is likely to be and plan ahead for their reaction. Is there any way that you can 'soften the blow' and have a transition between the current arrangements and what needs to happen next? Try to consider how you would react if you were the person receiving news. Might it be appropriate for you to signpost to your former partner that of the immediate issues to be resolved 'x' is, in your opinion, the most urgent issue to address. It may be a good idea to ask them to prioritise the immediate issues too as it will give you an indication of what you both need to sort first. It is highly likely that you will have different priorities!

Little people, little ears, long-term memories

Wherever possible remember that your children are just that. They are not mini-adults able to sympathise with your situation. In all likelihood they will be confused by why their parents are separating and fearful that they are in part to blame. Try to make it a golden rule that you do not discuss any areas of dispute in front of your children or when they are likely to hear those discussions. We recognise that this is a concept that it is easy to talk about but not so easy to do in practice. This rule applies whether your child is 3 or 13. The 13 year old may look like a mini adult but emotionally they are not and care needs to be taken not to overburden them with issues that they are not equipped to deal with.

Whilst it can be a good idea to put your thoughts into writing if you find it tricky to have a face-to-face discussion it can at times make a situation worse and not better. We have seen many cases where text messages or notes between former partners have been misconstrued. How many times have you received a message on your phone from someone where IT HAS BEEN TYPED IN CAPITALS? Is this simply that they are rubbish at text messaging and forgot it was being typed in capitals or were they sending a message intending to be 'shouted' at you.?

Text messaging can be enormously helpful if you are clarifying one quick point about collection time of a child later that day but only where you are already on good terms with each other. Otherwise, steer well clear of texts, emails and letters and direct all communications either at mediation or via your solicitors.

Paying for this at a time when you are both cross and angry can in the long run prove useful if it means that you are able to continue to communicate with your former partner long-term.

Beware of what you say online

Taking this a step further, beware of the ease with which you discuss your personal life online. Many people have social media accounts they frequently use. We regularly see cases where the use of Facebook, Snapchat or similar is causing problems. Whilst the Judges may not be so 'hot' on how social media works, it can prove to be very damaging to your case if you have frequent 'updates' where you are negative about your former partner and their treatment of the children, or where you bemoan your inevitable sale of the family home. Many children have their own social media accounts. If you and your child are 'linked' be even more cautious about what you say online. We encountered a case recently where a child was able to see their Father's updates and he had been negative about Mum's attitude towards contact. Not good. If in doubt, do not post anything on social networking sites as the chances are your ex will see it and if you are even the slightest bit negative about them it has the potential to cause a lot of upset, anger and hurt.

What about the children?

All too often we as lawyers ask the initial question of 'how are the children' and we are met with a response of 'they seem to be ok'. On the surface this may be so. However, the statistics tell us another story. For example, of the children that run away from home, a high percentage of them will be from a home when their parents have separated. Children's progress at school is frequently affected when their parents separate, and some children behave in a way which they previously had never displayed. For example, your child becoming withdrawn or argumentative at school. We as lawyers need to do more to ask you as the client what is important to you in terms of achieving stability for your children. You in turn need to help your lawyer by being clear about what you think your children need putting in place. As adults we know the reasons why the relationship has broken down but that information is not always communicated clearly to the children involved, leading them to speculate whether it was something that they did which caused the relationship to fail.

Many parents acknowledge to their children that separation from their former partner is an 'adult issue' and nothing to do with the way that a child has behaved. The children need to be aware of how things will change for them on a practical basis. Will they split their time between 2 homes and when will that take place? Will they still continue with their after-school activities and if so who will take them there and pay for them? What arrangements are going to be put in place to make sure that they always have school uniform and PE kit in the right place? Will they still be able to see their friends and socialise – particularly important to elder children.

If possible, sit with your children together and tell them of your decision to separate. Try to think of things from your child's point of view and address what you think will be their immediate concerns and be clear about how they will continue to see you both and where they will live in the short, medium and long term.

If you don't know, it's ok to say that you don't know because there are some things that still need to be discussed. The discussion needs to be age appropriate and clear. Think about the language that you intend to use. It may be a good idea for you and your former partner to agree beforehand what you are going to say and possibly get outside help if there are issues you are concerned about. Depending on the age of your children they may tell you then and there what their concerns are or they may become clear over the next few weeks and months. Inform your child's school and make sure that they are aware of the changes happening at home so that you can be informed if their behaviour changes. It may be that your child feels confident talking to their teacher about their concerns. If you already have a good relationship with the school it will ensure that the information comes to you as soon as possible.

Practical steps to take with the school

You will need to ask the school to amend their contact details so that copies of any letters, school reports and event notifications are sent to you both at your individual addresses. This might seem obvious but you would be surprised how many times we meet parents who have not received a copy of their child's school report and it then builds more resentment against their former partner where they feel they are ill-informed about their child's schooling. Schools are very used to dealing with parents who have separated and whilst you may find it upsetting to have this discussion with the school as it makes public the fact that you are separating it is a necessary discussion to have early on if you are going to be able to support your child.

Getting the children to talk

Relate have a section of their website aimed at young adults and children and can have counselling too. Their website www.relate.org.uk also has lots of useful information and tips for dealing with parents that are separating.

There are also other child-based counselling sessions run all over the country. The ideal is that both parents attend with their child so that you as parents understand more about how your child may be responding but you are given support to develop ways of communicating with each other so that you can co-parent. Children are put into age appropriate groups and given the practical support that they need both from their peers and fully qualified counsellors. The aim is to reduce the fear that children feel and reduce as much as possible their anxiety.

If a course is not for you, maybe your children feel able to talk to their peers or perhaps grandparents about their concerns and fears. The first hurdle is to get the children to accept that they have concerns. The next step is to get the help they require whether that be more support from you as their parents or from outside agencies. We often find that initially the children react ok, but as the impact of their parents separating takes effect and the practical things start to change (like selling the family home or one parent moving out of the house) that is when the cracks start to show.

Ensure that your children know they can talk to you when they are ready. In our busy lives it is easy to be distracted when having conversations with our children. Try to make sure that if your children do want to talk to you that they have your full attention, your mobile phone is nowhere near to you and you are not trying to cook at the same time!

Key dates

Where possible agree at the outset what key dates are important to each of you. It is often said that you are a parent for life – not just until they are 18. It is also sadly true that you are unlikely to be able to continue the family traditions you both had when living together. Christmas holidays, summer holidays and birthday celebrations will evolve until you find you have begun new traditions. Remember though that whilst it is hard to think of 'missing out' on your child's Christmas Day experience one year, the same will be true for your former partner the following year. If you have a consensus about how you will deal with the important dates in your family diaries at the outset it will save a lot of time, money and heartache later on.

We lawyers know only too well the outcome of a contested Christmas contact case and although we can say to people at the outset that the court is likely to allocate alternate Christmases to you both, in all honesty by the time the cases reach us it is often too late to talk sense. Tempers have risen and positions firmly adopted.

Review

Parents often say to their lawyers that they want to review the arrangements they have put in place for their children when a relationship ends and to see whether things need changing after the initial hiatus when one parents moves out of the family home. Of course this is important but it isn't the only review that is needed.

More often than not the receipt of a Decree Absolute can result in tears and although we as lawyers warn our clients that separating is an emotional process and there are ups and downs people seem often ill-prepared for the obvious.

Another time when the reality of the separation hits home is if your former partner announces their intention to remarry or perhaps they are having a baby with their new partner. Whilst life moves on whether we want it to or not, the receipt of this information often sends even the most 'together' person to pieces. It is never too late to receive counselling. Sometimes those who have shunned the idea of counselling throughout the separation process turn to it at the end. It is almost as if it would have been a sign of weakness to admit they needed outside help during the legal proceedings but once they have reached an agreement and sorted the paperwork receiving outside help is more acceptable.

If you find yourself feeling more 'wobbly' about the separation once matters are coming to an end keep in your head the idea that counselling is available and helpful. Whilst paying for counselling in addition to any money spent on lawyers is probably going to be the last thing you really want to invest in it is just that – an investment. If you don't get yourself sorted – nobody else can do it for you!

Now read the main points from Chapter 10 overleaf.

****

Main Points from Chapter 10

Moving on

➢ The decision to move forwards and establish a different type of relationship with your former partner is not easy and for some people it will continue to be a challenge many years after they have separated.

➢ The key to a successful transition is to get it right at the beginning. This will also impact on how much you will eventually spend on lawyers.

➢ If you have children together it is even more important to sort out the emotional issues early on.

➢ Consider carefully your methods of communication and how you choose to communicate. Try to keep clear of sending texts or using social networking sites. Manage your communication successfully in order to limit any future problems.

****

Chapter 11

Resources

- Summary of expenditure
- Preparation questions
- Useful addresses
- Useful websites

Summary of Expenditure

Schedule of outgoings Item	Present Expense	Estimated Expense	Explanatory note if applicable
Personal Finance Costs			
Pension			
Private medical insurance			
Credit cards			
Loan repayments (not including car loan)			
Other financial payments			
Hire purchase			
TOTAL			

Housing Costs			
Mortgage			
Rent			
Ground rent			
Service charge			
Council tax			
Water rates			
Gas			
Oil			
Other fuels			
Electricity			
Telephone (land line)			
Telephone (mobile)			
Buildings insurance			
Contents insurance			
Repairs/maintenance			
Service contracts			
Maintenance of central heating			
Whole life policy premiums			
Endowment policy premiums			
Mortgage protection policy			
Total			

Schedule of Outgoings Item	Present Expense	Estimated Expense	Explanatory note if applicable
Car maintenance			
Car insurance			
AA/RAC			
Petrol/diesel			
Servicing			
Repairs			
MOT			
Depreciation			
Car loan			
TOTAL			
Schedule of outgoings Item	**Present Expense**	**Estimated Expense**	**Explanatory note if applicable**
Domestic expenses			
Food and housekeeping			
Domestic help			
Window cleaning			
Gardner			
Garden plants, seeds etc.			
Pet food			
Vet Bills			
Animal insurance			
Total			

Schedule of outgoings Item	Present expense	Estimated Expense	Explanatory notes if applicable
Personal expenses			
Clothing			
Shoes			
Lunches at work			
Travelling to work			
Travel expenses not covered elsewhere			
Doctor/prescriptions			
Optician			
Personal toiletries			
Hairdressing			
Dentist			
Laundry			
Beautician			
Other			
TV/cable /Licence			
Magazines and newspapers			
Social entertainment			
Gym/other			
Holidays			
Presents (Christmas and birthdays)			
Miscellaneous			
TOTAL			

Schedule of outgoings Item	Present expense	Estimated expense	Explanatory notes if applicable
Replacement items			
Replacement household items			
Replacement furniture			
Tools for work			
Professional fees not paid by employer			
TOTAL			
Schedule of outgoings item	**Present expense**	**Estimated expense**	**Explanatory note if applicable**
Maintenance liabilities			
Maintenance payments for ex-spouse/children			
TOTAL			
Schedule of outgoings Item	**Present expense**	**Estimated expense**	**Explanatory note if applicable**
Children			
School fees			
Nursery expenses			
Nanny/childminder			

Babysitter			
Travel to and from school			
School uniform			
School shoes			
Other clothing			
Sports equipment			
Sports activities			
Other out of school activities/expenses			
Equipment for above			
Nappies			
Toys			
Pocket money			
Books/magazines/ stationery etc.			
Christmas and birthday expenses not included under 'presents' elsewhere'			
Gifts for birthday parties			
Presents 'from' the children			
Trips out e.g. cinema, zoo etc)			
Extra lessons			
Clubs, subscriptions,			

fees etc			
School trips			
Holidays			
Holiday treats and outings			
Sweets etc			
Dentist			
Other			
Total			
Summary of total expenditure from above	**Current**	**Future if different**	**Explanatory note if applicable**
Personal finance costs			
Housing costs			
Car expenses			
Domestic expenses			
Personal expenses			
Replacement items			
Maintenance			
Children			
Total			

****

Useful information

The following are some of the more useful addresses and web sites.

Asian Family Counselling Service (London)
4 Triangle Centre
399 Uxbridge Road
Southall
Middlesex
UB1 3EJ
Tel: 0208 574 0912
Email: afcs@btconnect.com

West Midlands
1 Hampton Court, George Road, Edgbaston
Birmingham B15 1PU
0121 454 1130
Email:bham.afcs@btconnect.com

Association for Shared Parenting
0300 121 0131
Email: info@sharedparentingorg.co.uk

Rudlings Wakelam Solicitors 14 Woolhall Street Bury St Edmunds IP33 1LA01284 755771
elisabeth.sneade@rudlings-wakelam.com

Child Maintenance Options
www.cmoptions.org

0800 083 4375

Welsh language 0800 408 0308

www.gov.uk

Child Poverty Action Group

30 Micawber Street

London N1 7TB

Tel: 020 7837 7979

Web site: cpag.org.uk

Coram

41 Brunswick Square,

London WC1 1AZ

www.coram.org.uk

020 7520 0300

Family Mediation Council

International Dispute Resolution Centre

70 Fleet Street

London EC4Y 1EY

Tel: 01707 594055

9am-3pm Monday to Friday

familymediationcouncil.org.uk

Gingerbread

0207 428 5400

54 -74 Holmes Road

London NW5 3AQ.

Web site: www.gingerbread.org.uk. A support organisation for lone parents and their families, with around 20 centres.

Institute of Family law Arbitrators (IFLA)
www.ifla.org.uk

National Family Mediation
Civic Centre
Paris Street
Exeter
Devon EX1 1JN
0300 4000 636
www.nfm.org.uk

Women's Aid
PO Box 3245
Bristol BS2 2EH
National Domestic Abuse Helpline
0808 2000 247
24hr DomesticViolence Helpline

Relate
National Phoneline 0300 100 1234
email relate.enquiries@relate.org.uk
Website: www.relate.org.uk

Relate Cymru
0300 003 2340
enquiries@relate.cymru.org.uk

Resolution
General enquiries 020 3841 0300 email:info@resolution.org.uk

Scottish Women's Aid
132 Rose Street
Edinburgh EH2 3JD
0800 027 1234-Helpline @sdafmh.org.uk
womensaid.scot

Useful websites
www.rudlings-wakelam.com
www.janemccann.co.uk

www.resolution.org.uk
www.landregistry.gov.uk
www.moneyadviceservice.org.uk

the www.gov.uk website has access to information from all government agencies, including child maintenance, benefit entitlement, pensions, court forms, court applications and forms and also legal aid.

www.ifla.org.
www.parentingpeople.co.uk/
www.relate.org.uk/
www.divorceandchildren.com
www.cafcass.gov.uk
actionforchildren.org.uk

Preparation questions

Ask yourself these questions as you embark on the process of separation and divorce.

- Is it what I really want?

- What do I want from my new life?

- What don't I want from my new life?

- What is really important to me?

- What matters most and what matters least?

- What do our children need from us?

- How will you fund your legal costs?

- What do I need from my ex and

- What can I offer them?

- Looking back in 2/5/10 years time, would I want to reflect on how I coped with this point of my life?

- What's the best that I can do?

****

RECOMMENDED READING

1. It's not your fault Koko Bear – a read together book for parents and young children during divorce.
   Vicky Lansky and Jane Prince. Meadowbrook Press

2. Dinosaur's Divorce. A guide for changing families.
   Laurence Krasny Brown and Marc Brown.
   Littlebrown

3. Clean Break by Jacqueline Wilson (age 9+)
   Yearling Books

4. Helping Children Cope with Divorce (Overcoming common problems) by Rosemary Wells
   Sheldon Press

5. Help your children cope with divorce – a relate guide by Paula Hall
   Vermillion Press

6. Great answers to difficult questions about divorce. What children need to know by Fanny Cohen Herlem.
   Jessica Kingsley Books

7. Putting children first ; A handbook for separated parents by Karen and Nick Woodall. Piatkus Books

8. Gary Bailey's Divorce for Dads: making the right choices for your kids by Gary Bailey and Nick Woodall
   Two Dogs

9. Parenting Apart: How Separated and Divorced Parents Can Raise and Leave Kids-Christina McGee
   Vermilion

. 10. Mom's House Dad's House: A Complete Guide for parent's who are divorced or living apart.
   Isolina Ricci PHD
   Fireside Books

****

Index

Emerald Guides

Other titles in the Emerald Series:

Law
Guide to Bankruptcy
Conducting Your Own Court case
Guide to Consumer law
Creating a Will
Guide to Family Law
Guide to Employment Law
Guide to European Union Law
Guide to Health and Safety Law
Guide to Criminal Law
Guide to Landlord and Tenant Law
Guide to the English Legal System
Guide to Housing Law
Guide to Marriage and Divorce
Guide to The Civil Partnerships Act
Guide to The Law of Contract
The Path to Justice
You and Your Legal Rights

Health
Guide to Combating Child Obesity
Asthma Begins at Home
Stop Smoking Now
Understanding Depression and Stress
Explaining Bi-Polar Disorder
Self Hypnosis and Positive Affirmations

Music

How to Survive and Succeed in the Music Industry

General

A Practical Guide to Obtaining probate

A Practical Guide to Residential Conveyancing

Writing The Perfect CV

Keeping Books and Accounts-A Small Business Guide

Business Start Up-A Guide for New Business

Finding Asperger Syndrome in the Family-A Book of Answers

Explaining Autism

Explaining Dementia and Alzheimers

For details of the above titles published under Emerald guides go to:

www.straightforwardco.co.uk

****